MADRID

ENCOUNTER

ANTHONY HAM

Madrid Encounter
Published by Lonely Planet Publications Pty Ltd
ABN 36 005 607 983

Australia	Head Office, Locked Bag 1, Footscray, Vic 3011
	☎ 03 8379 8000 fax 03 8379 8111
	talk2us@lonelyplanet.com.au
USA	150 Linden St, Oakland, CA 94607
	☎ 510 893 8555
	toll free 800 275 8555
	fax 510 893 8572
	info@lonelyplanet.com
UK	2nd fl, 186 City Rd, London EC1V 2NT
	☎ 020 7106 2100 fax 020 7106 2101
	go@lonelyplanet.co.uk

This title was commissioned in Lonely Planet's London office and produced by: **Commissioning Editor** Lucy Monie **Coordinating Editor** Shawn Low **Coordinating Cartographer** Valeska Cañas **Layout Designer** Paul Iacono **Assisting Editor** Kate Evans **Assisting Cartographer** Joanne Luke **Managing Editor** Annelies Mertens **Managing Cartographer** Alison Lyall **Cover** Image research provided by lonelyplanetimages.com **Project Manager** Chris Girdler **Thanks to** Sally Darmody, Melanie Dankel, Laura Jane, Lyahna Spencer

Our Readers Many thanks to the travellers who wrote to us with helpful hints, useful advice and interesting anecdotes:Yeshwanti Balagopal, Candice Barnett, Richard Brooker, Joy Jaffe, Steven Johnstone, Evelyn Kimber, Patricia Nelson, Mr & Mrs O'Neil, Eric Paya, Karen Ramsay, Martijn Roelandse, Teresa, John Thompson, Susan Trout

ISBN 978 1 74104 672 4

Printed through Colorcraft Ltd, Hong Kong.
Printed in China.

Acknowledgement Madrid Metro Map © Diseño Raro S.L. 2009.

Lonely Planet and the Lonely Planet logo are trademarks of Lonely Planet and are registered in the US Patent and Trademark Office and in other countries.

Lonely Planet does not allow its name or logo to be appropriated by commercial establishments, such as retailers, restaurants or hotels. Please let us know of any misuses: www.lonelyplanet.com/ip.

HOW TO USE THIS BOOK
Colour-Coding & Maps

Colour-coding is used for symbols on maps and in the text that they relate to (eg all eating venues on the maps and in the text are given a green fork symbol). Each neighbourhood also gets its own colour, and this is used down the edge of the page and throughout that neighbourhood section.

Shaded yellow areas on the maps denote 'areas of interest' – for their historical significance, their attractive architecture or their great bars and restaurants. We encourage you to head to these areas and just start exploring!

Send us your feedback We love to hear from readers – your comments help make our books better. We read every word you send us, and we always guarantee that your feedback goes straight to the appropriate authors. The most useful submissions are rewarded with a free book. To send us your updates and find out about Lonely Planet events, newsletters and travel news visit our award-winning website: *lonelyplanet .com/contact*.

Note: We may edit, reproduce and incorporate your comments in Lonely Planet products such as guidebooks, websites and digital products, so let us know if you don't want your comments reproduced or your name acknowledged. For a copy of our privacy policy visit *lonelyplanet.com/privacy*.

ANTHONY HAM

After years of wandering the world, Anthony has finally found his spiritual home in Madrid. In 2001, Anthony watched spellbound as the Puerta del Sol thronged with energy and people, and the Plaza Mayor came alive with street musicians and all the languages of the world. In that moment, he fell irretrievably in love with the city. Less than a year later, Anthony arrived in Madrid on a one-way ticket, with not a word of Spanish and not knowing a single person in the city. Just a few years later, Anthony speaks Spanish with a Madrileño accent, is married to Marina, a Madrileña, and their daughter Carlota was born in Madrid in August 2007. Together they live in an apartment overlooking their favourite plaza in Madrid. When he's not writing for Lonely Planet, Anthony writes on Madrid for a number of newspapers and magazines around the world.

ANTHONY'S THANKS

Muchísimas gracias to Juan Manuel Herrero (Turismo Madrid) – Madrid has no finer ambassador. Special thanks also to Agatha Ruiz de la Prada, Lola Moriarty and Giles Tremlett for being so generous with their time. Thanks also to Raul, Dolores, Carolina, Jota, James, Eva and Richard Foster. And to Marina and Carlota: may all your dreams come true in this wonderful city.

THE PHOTOGRAPHER

Born and raised in Warsaw, Krzysztof Dydyński discovered a passion for travelling, which took him on various trips across Europe, Asia, South America, and finally to Australia where he now lives. He first visited Spain in 1974 and has returned regularly ever since. Madrid is one of his favourite cities, where he has been back time and again, revisiting his old secret corners and looking for new inspirations.

Cover photograph Tapas bar in Puerta del Sol, Herve Hughes/Photolibrary. **Internal photographs** p26 & 27 by IFEMA, p63 Dennis Doyle, p111 courtesy of Galeria Moriarty. All other photographs by Lonely Planet Images, and by Krzysztof Dydyński except p29 Juliet Coombe; p12, p30 Guy Moberly; p14, p91 Richard Nebesky; p25 Damien Simonis.

All images are copyright of the photographers unless otherwise indicated. Many of the images in this guide are available for licensing from **Lonely Planet Images:** www.lonelyplanetimages.com

Edificio Metrópolis (p41), Calle de Alcala

CONTENTS

THIS IS MADRID

Madrid is an ex-convent schoolgirl, a rebellious teenager who pushed the boundaries of hedonism and then grew up and got sophisticated without ever forgetting how to have fun. That's why this is a city as at home in the nightclubs and bars that give the streets their soundtrack as it is in the hallowed halls of high culture.

It's true that Spain's capital doesn't have the immediate cachet of Rome, Paris or even that other city up the road, Barcelona. Its architecture is beautiful, but there's no Colosseum, no Eiffel Tower, no Gaudí-inspired zaniness to photograph and then tell your friends back home, 'this is Madrid'. But this city is an idea, a way of living for the moment that can be hard to resist.

Madrid's calling cards are many – astonishing art galleries; dynamic and relentless nightlife; the sophistication and variety of the life coursing through the streets or reclining in the city's plazas; its extraordinary and relatively recent transformation into Spain's premier style city; a burgeoning live flamenco and jazz music scene; a feast of fine restaurants and tapas bars; and a population that's mastered the art of living the good life. It's not that other cities don't have some of these things. It's just that Madrid has all of them in bucketloads.

It's often said that this is the most Spanish of Spain's cities and it is indeed Europe's most passionate city writ large. Very few Madrileños come from here originally, possibly making this Europe's most open and welcoming capital. If this can be summed up in a single phrase, it's the oft-heard, 'If you're in Madrid, you're from Madrid'. It's not that they'll knock you over with the warmth of their welcome. Rather, you'll find yourself in a bar or lost somewhere and in need of directions, and you'll suddenly be made to feel like one of their own. Just as quickly, without knowing when it happened, you'll realise that you never want to leave.

Top left Too much colour is never enough at Agatha Ruíz de la Prada (p91) **Top right** Cruising locals in the Parque del Buen Retiro (p17) **Bottom** Drink yourself back to the '80s and *la movida madrileña* (Madrid Movement) at La Vía Láctea (p124)

A flamenco show ignites the night in Casa Patas (p69)

>1 PLAZA MAYOR

WATCH THE PASSING PARADE IN PLAZA MAYOR

For centuries the centrepiece of Madrid life, the stately Plaza Mayor combines supremely elegant architecture with a history dominated by peculiarly Spanish dramas. Pull up a chair at the outdoor tables around the perimeter or laze upon the rough-hewn cobblestones as young Madrileños have a habit of doing. All around you, the theatre that is Spanish street-life coursing through the plaza provides a crash course in why people fall in love with Madrid.

First laid out in 1619, the plaza won the hearts of Madrileños from the beginning by hosting the beatification of the city's patron saint, San Isidro Labrador. Until 1790 the macabre rituals of the Spanish Inquisition took over (burnings at the stake and deaths by garrotte on the north side of the square, hangings to the south) until fire consumed the plaza. Then, until 1878, up to 50,000 people would cram into the square for bullfights.

As you ponder this, you may quickly come to the conclusion that this is one of Spain's most beautiful plazas with its slate spires and stunningly uniform ochre-and-wrought-iron façades. The Real Casa de la Panadería is the standout feature among many – the extraordinary frescoes (created in the 1990s during restorations) which adorn the façade on the plaza's northern side glitter in the sunlight or glow with an otherworldly brilliance when floodlit by night. See also p44.

>2 EL RASTRO

HUNT FOR TREASURE AT SUNDAY'S EL RASTRO MARKET

To call El Rastro the largest flea market in Europe is to tell only half its story. This is one of Madrid's most enduring traditions, a place where Madrileños from all walks of life come together to edge their way through the crowds, bargain for cheap clothes or household kitsch and pick their way through the junk for a real treasure – every now and then an original Picasso or Goya turns up here. Even El Rastro's name (which means 'the stain'; this was once Madrid's main meat market and the name refers to the trail of blood left behind by animals dragged down the hill) lends the place a certain earthy charm. Inching your way down the Ribera de los Curtidores (Tanners' Alley) is sometimes overwhelming, sometimes exhilarating, but El Rastro's charm extends beyond the market's sprawling confines. If you're a true Madrileño, a morning at El Rastro is a prelude to a day spent in an ever-widening arc of tapas bars, eating and drinking to your heart's content. See also p62.

>3 MUSEO DEL PRADO

BE OVERWHELMED BY GOYA AND VELÁZQUEZ AT THE MUSEO DEL PRADO

You could come to Madrid just to see the Museo del Prado and not leave disappointed, for few galleries in the world can boast such a rich collection of masterpieces. Adorning the walls in the neoclassical, 18th-century Palacio de Villanueva are more than 3000 paintings (less than half of the entire 7000-painting collection) by the great Spanish and wider European masters. A recent major overhaul of the gallery has added a whole new wing, the Edificio Jerónimos, which contains delightful 17th-century cloisters, temporary exhibition space, the gallery shop and a café.

Lest you find yourself overwhelmed by this sumptuous artistic feast, two Spanish painters – the imperious Velázquez and the disturbing Goya, each in their own way without peer – should provide the focus for your visit. The royal portraits that made Diego Rodríguez de Silva y Velázquez (1599–1660) famous fill rooms 12, 14, 15 and 16 and every one of them seems to glower down from the walls, at once compelling and vivid and always filled with personality and life. *Las Meninas*, arguably Velázquez's signature work, is in room 36. Completed in 1656, it is more properly known as *La Família de*

Felipe IV (The Family of Felipe IV) and the painter's mastery of light and colour is extraordinary.

Francisco José de Goya y Lucientes (1746–1828) is the other towering figure of the Prado, with paintings that chart the easily scandalised, tortured Spanish soul of the early 19th century. In room 22, his *La Maja Vestida* and *La Maja Desnuda* tell of Goya's rumoured (and scandalous) love affair with the Duquesa de Alba. There are no more dramatic paintings in the Prado than *El Dos de Mayo* and *El Tres de Mayo* (room 65), which bring to life the 1808 anti-French revolt and subsequent execution of insurgents in Madrid. Evidence that there is little in the Prado that leaves the visitor unmoved comes amid the unsettling works of Goya's later years, the *Pinturas Negras* (Black Paintings) in room 67 where you'll both marvel at and recoil from the dark vision of the old Spanish master.

Titian, Tintoretto, El Greco, Francisco de Zurbarán, José de Ribera, Peter Paul Rubens, Anton Van Dyck, Rembrandt, Botticelli and Albrecht Dürer are also sprinkled lightly throughout, but it's a mark of the Prado's extravagance that these can all seem secondary to the gallery's appeal. Seek them all out, but on no account miss *The Garden of Earthly Delights* by Dutch painter Hieronymus Bosch (1450–1516) in room 56A; it's one of the most surreal works committed to canvas. See also p84.

>4 PLAZA DE ORIENTE

RUB SHOULDERS WITH ROYALTY IN THE PLAZA DE ORIENTE

A royal palace that once had aspirations to be the Spanish Versailles. Sophisticated cafés watched over by apartments that cost the equivalent of a royal salary. The Teatro Real – Madrid's opera house and one of Spain's temples to high culture. Some of the finest sunset views in Madrid. Welcome to Plaza de Oriente, a living, breathing monument to imperial Madrid.

When a castle built by the city's founders burned down in 1734, Felipe V set about building the Palacio Real (Royal Palace), which he hoped would dwarf all its European counterparts. The 2800-room Italianate baroque colossus never quite scaled such heights, but its soaring white façade is magnificent, as are the 50 rooms that are open to the public; the highlights are the Farmacia Real (Royal Pharmacy), Armería Real (Royal Armoury), royal apartments, Sala de Porcelana (Porcelain Room), silk-walled Salón de Gasparini and the Salón del Trono (Throne Room) with its Tiepolo ceiling and crimson-velvet wall coverings.

Perhaps embarrassed by the extravagance of it all, Spain's current ruling family lives elsewhere in more modest surrounds, coming here only for official receptions.

At the centre of the plaza that the palace overlooks is an equestrian statue of Felipe IV. Designed by Velázquez, it's the perfect place for marvellous views wherever you look. Nearby are some 20 marble statues of mostly ancient monarchs. Legend has it that these ageing royals get down off their pedestals at night to stretch their legs.

The palace and other signposts of royalty give Plaza de Oriente its grandeur; the street performers and strolling crowds that throng here by day and night give the plaza its personality. Violinists provide a Bach or Mozart soundtrack. The changing of the guard at noon on the first Wednesday of the month (except July and August), between the palace and the Catedral de Nuestra Señora de la Almudena, provides colour away to the south. And in fine weather, crowds flock to the delightful Jardines Cabo Naval at the plaza's northern end to watch the sun set over the perfectly manicured Jardines de Sabatini. The whole effect is agreeable in a way that only Madrid can be. See also p44.

>5 CENTRO DE ARTE REINA SOFÍA

BE UPLIFTED BY PICASSO'S GUERNICA AT THE CENTRO DE ARTE REINA SOFÍA

Salvador Dalí, Joan Miró, Wassily Kandinsky, Federico García Lorca, Francis Bacon, Henry Moore and Eduardo Chillida should be sufficient reason to visit the Centro de Arte Reina Sofía. But as important as these eminent masters are, it is Pablo Picasso who casts a shadow over them all. Above all else, it is Picasso's *Guernica* that the crowds come to see.

One of the most famous paintings of the 20th century, *Guernica* is a signature work of cubism whose disfiguration of the human form became an eloquent symbol of the world's outrage at the horrors wrought upon the innocent by modern warfare. Measuring 3.5m by 7.8m, *Guernica* was Picasso's riposte to the bombing of Gernika (Guernica) in the Basque Country by Hitler's Legión Condor, at the request of Franco, on 26 April 1937; almost 2000 people died in the attack. The painting was, Picasso said, to 'express my abhorrence of the military caste which has sunk Spain in an ocean of pain and death'. Never has an artist's anger and a people's anguish been so movingly committed to canvas. See also p72.

>6 PARQUE DEL BUEN RETIRO

STROLL AMONG THE SUNDAY CROWDS IN THE PARQUE DEL BUEN RETIRO

If it's Sunday and the weather's fine, all of Madrid comes out to play at the Parque del Buen Retiro. It's not that 'El Retiro' can't be enjoyed on other days. It's just that on Sundays it overflows with street performers, impromptu drumming-and-dance parties, picnicking families and lovers taking a boat out onto the lake, but still has enough space for you to find a shady patch of lawn all to yourself.

No ordinary park, this luxuriant expanse of green in the heart of Madrid was once the private preserve of kings and queens and they left behind a legacy of stunning architectural showpieces. The lake is watched over by the ornamental Monumento de Alfonso XII on the east side, complete with marble lions, while the Palacio de Cristal is a charming metal-and-glass structure hidden among the trees. In the park's northeastern corner lie the 13th-century Romanesque ruins of the Ermita de San Isidro, while the southwestern corner is home to the poignant Bosque de los Ausentes, an olive-and-cypress-tree memorial to the 191 victims of the 11 March 2004 train bombings. Near La Rosaleda (Rose Gardens) at the southern end of the park, the statue of *El Ángel Caído* (The Fallen Angel) is one of the few statues to the devil anywhere in the world. See also p85.

>7 CHUECA

EAT AND PARTY TO YOUR HEART'S CONTENT IN GAY CHUECA

Not that long ago, Chueca was a neglected inner-city barrio (neighbourhood) of tumbledown buildings, rampant crime and ghettoised poverty. Seeing Chueca's potential, scores of young gay professionals moved into the area and dragged the barrio up by its bootstraps. Apartments, then buildings, then whole blocks were renovated, often with the rainbow flag of the gay movement draped from the balconies. Calle de la Libertad became (and remains) famous for hip restaurants. The bars and nightclubs occupying an ever-widening circle of streets around the Plaza de Chueca were (and are) a starting point for the roar of the night-time crowd that booms out across the city. And down on Calle de Piamonte, heartbreakingly stylish boutiques, like so many niche outposts of Salamanca, have similarly proved that they're here to stay. The combination means that Chueca is now one of the most upwardly mobile barrios in Madrid, a leading contender for the title of nightlife capital and as optimistic a place as you'll find in this city. In short, Chueca is Madrid in microcosm: sophisticated, tolerant, inclusive and always living for the moment. See also p102.

>8 CALLE DE SERRANO

SHOP FOR THE LATEST SPANISH DESIGNS ON CALLE DE SERRANO

Madrid's Calle de Serrano may just be the most glamorous street in Spain. Running like a river through the heart of Salamanca, stately Calle de Serrano has drawn the pick of Spain's innovative designers to its banks. From the colourful Agatha Ruiz de la Prada to Loewe (Spain's answer to Louis Vuitton), from the fun designs of Camper footwear to Manolo Blahnik whose shoes are considered works of art. Those unable to find room along the street have drawn close; an address on Calle de Claudio Coello or Callejón de Jorge Juan is equally prestigious. Put on your finest clothes. Be seen. And above all, promenade like a true fashionista. Calle de Serrano is in the process of becoming even more beautiful: major works (due to be completed in 2011) are underway with wider footpaths and more trees planned. See also p91.

HIGHLIGHTS

>9 ESTADIO SANTIAGO BERNABÉU

CHEER THE GALÁCTICOS OF REAL MADRID AT THE ESTADIO SANTIAGO BERNABÉU

If sport has its temples then Madrid's Estadio Santiago Bernabéu is football's spiritual home. Real Madrid, voted the world's greatest football club of all time by FIFA in 1998, has won a peerless nine European Cups or Champions Leagues (including in 1998, 2000 and 2002) as well as 31 Spanish Liga titles and a host of other trophies. As a result, the club's Exposición de Trofeos (Trophy Exhibition) is like nothing you've ever seen before. But Real Madrid is as much about glamour as it is about football success, and cheering on the latest crop of *galácticos* (big-name player imports) surrounded by 80,000 Madridistas (Real Madrid supporters) is a spine-tingling experience and one of the most memorable moments you'll have in sport. After a trophy-less 2008–09 season, the arrival of a new crop of *galácticos* in the summer of 2009 has created a frisson of excitement around the club, making it clear that the potent mix of celebrity and the cachet of the Real Madrid shirt and stadium continues to captivate the world. You'll never forget a visit here. See also p90.

>10 MALASAÑA
RETURN TO THE HEDONISM OF 1980S MADRID IN MALASAÑA

If the spirit of those endless Madrid nights of hedonism during *la movida madrileña* (sociocultural movement in the years after the death of Francisco Franco) in the 1980s lives on, it does so in Malasaña. In this tangle of narrow streets, a retro crowd spills from bars and from the Plaza de Dos de Mayo while DJs and live rock bands pay homage to the '80s and to the spirit of 'if you're not hurting anyone, do whatever you like' that so defined *la movida*. Forget for a night the House music and the bars that serve as temples to minimalist chic, which have increasingly come to define the Spanish capital's world-famous nightlife. Malasaña is the enduring soul of the Madrid night with places such as La Vía Láctea awash with sideburns, hair gel and that unmistakable feel-good vibe that Madrid does so well. See also p114.

>11 HUERTAS

EXPERIENCE THE PASSION OF FLAMENCO OR JAZZ IN HUERTAS

Huertas is one of Madrid's emblematic nightlife barrios, illuminating the night with a choice of bars, restaurants and nightclubs as overwhelming as the crowds that flow through the barrio's streets. Plaza de Santa Ana is the barrio's centrepiece and its popularity has made Huertas nights the most international in Madrid, a place where the world comes to party alongside many a Madrileño of longer standing. But the secret of Huertas, tucked away in the back streets of the barrio, is some of Madrid's best and most intimate live music.

Flamenco's roots may lie in Andalucía, but Madrid is fast becoming the city of choice for established and up-and-coming flamenco artists keen to make their name beyond Sevilla or Jerez de la Frontera. There are *tablaos* (restaurants with a flamenco floorshow) across Madrid, and the Festival Flamenco is played out in major venues across the capital. But Huertas is where you get flamenco at its best in smoky bars crowded with knowledgeable flamenco aficionados. Cardamomo

(p80), on Calle de Echegaray, is just such a place, one that people-in-the-know consider one of the most authentic of Madrid's flamenco venues. Nightly *cantaor* (flamenco singers) and guitarists bring the spontaneity of a flamenco session alive as audiences crowd the tiny stage. The effect will send chills down your spine and you'll come away uplifted by music that speaks straight to the soul. The iconic Villa Rosa (p81), on Plaza de Santa Ana, is another outstanding flamenco stage.

As for flamenco, so too for jazz. With such riches on offer, it's difficult to choose favourites, but Café Central (p80), on Calle de las Huertas, is one of the world's premier jazz venues and a regular on the prestigious European jazz circuit, with an Art Deco interior thrown in for good measure. Nearby, Populart (p80) also draws world-class acts that add to the complementary cross rhythms that nightly ring out across Huertas. Down the Huertas hill, Jazz Bar (p78) is like a mellow after-party for aficionados after the live venues fall quiet. Perhaps best of all, getting swept up in the moment here – as you tend to do in Madrid – means making new friends who may initiate you into more Huertas secrets and that Huertas speciality – nights that never seem to end. See also p70.

>12 CALLE DE LA CAVA BAJA
CATCH THE FEEL-GOOD VIBE ALONG CALLE DE LA CAVA BAJA

You've visited the Plaza Mayor. You've had your fill of art at the Museo del Prado. Now it's time to embrace the wonderful world of eating and drinking Madrid-style. No street can compete with Calle de la Cava Baja, whose medieval façades mark the site of the city walls that once surrounded old Madrid. Lined with tapas bars, restaurants and places serving every drink you could wish for, the street's gentle curve is a bridge between the earthy charms of Sunday's El Rastro flea market and the grandeur of the Plaza Mayor. As such, it's a thoroughfare that is a Madrid favourite, especially on Sunday, for a tipple and a plate of tapas at places such as Txakolina (p66) and Casa Lucas (p64). But any bar, any restaurant along here is a classic. See also p58.

>MADRID DIARY

Madrid never needs an excuse to party but there are organised fiestas to provide order to the chaos. The best source of information is the Centro de Turismo de Madrid (p168). Its monthly *esMadrid Magazine* (www.esmadrid.com) has major listings. Also try *Guía del Ocio* (www.guiadelocio.com/madrid), a €1 Spanish-language weekly magazine at news kiosks. The monthly English expat publication *In Madrid* (www.in-madrid.com) is given out free at some hotels, original-version cinemas, Irish pubs and English bookshops. *Le Cool* (www.lecool.com) also has its finger on the pulse.

Penitents in traditional costume, Easter procession (p27)

JANUARY

Año Nuevo (New Year)

On New Year's Eve *(noche vieja)*, Madrileños gather in Puerta del Sol to wait for the 12 *campanadas* (bell chimes), whereupon they try to stuff 12 grapes (one for each chime) into their mouths and make a wish for the New Year.

Reyes

The Día de los Reyes Magos (Three Kings' Day) on 6 January is when young Madrileños traditionally receive their presents. Three local politicians dress up and lead a sweet-distributing frenzy of horse-drawn carriages and floats (Cabalgata de Reyes) from the Parque del Buen Retiro to Plaza Mayor at 6pm on 5 January.

FEBRUARY

Carnaval

Several days of fancy-dress parades and merrymaking in many barrios across the Comunidad de Madrid, usually ending on the Tuesday 47 days before Easter Sunday.

Festival Flamenco Caja Madrid

A combination of big names and rising talent comes together for five days of fine flamenco music in the Teatros del Canal.

Arco

www.arco.ifema.es

One of Europe's biggest celebrations of contemporary art, the Feria Internacional de Arte Contemporánea draws galleries and exhibitors from all over the world.

Striking a pose at Arco contemporary-art festival

Back stage at Pasarela Cibeles fashion show

Pasarela Cibeles
www.cibeles.ifema.es, in Spanish
The Pasarela Cibeles, staged in the Feria de Madrid, is becoming an increasingly important stop on the European fashion circuit, especially for spring and autumn collections.

MARCH & APRIL

Jazz es Primavera
Madrid is known for its happening jazz scene and never more so than in March, with four weeks of jazz in venues across the city.

Jesús de Medinaceli
Up to 100,000 people crowd the Iglesia de Jesús de Medinaceli on the first Friday of Lent to kiss the right foot of a wooden sculpture of Christ.

Semana Santa (Easter)
Jueves Santo (Holy Thursday) sees local *cofradías* (lay fraternities) organise colourful and often solemn religious processions. Hooded men and barefoot women drag chains around their ankles and bear crosses through the streets, concluding by crossing the Plaza Mayor to the Basílica de Nuestra Señora del Buen Consejo.

MAY

Fiesta de la Comunidad de Madrid

On 2 May (El Dos de Mayo) in 1808, Napoleon's troops put down an uprising in Madrid, and commemoration of the day of Spanish struggle has become an opportunity for much festivity. The day is celebrated with particular energy in the bars of Malasaña.

Madrid Masters

www.madrid-open.com

The Madrid Masters in the first half of May draws many of the top names in tennis.

Fiestas de San Isidro

Madrid's big holiday is a celebration of the city's patron saint, San Isidro el Labrador. On 15 May Madrileños gather in central Madrid to watch the colourful procession that inaugurates a week of cultural events across the city. The festival marks the commencement of Spain's most prestigious *feria* (bullfighting season).

Festimad

www.festimad.es

Bands from all over the country and beyond converge on Móstoles (on the MetroSur train network) for two days of indie-music indulgence. Dates change each year (sometimes

Celebrate outdoors for the Fiestas de San Isidro

spilling over into April or June) so check the website.

JUNE

Fiesta de San Antonio

Young Madrileñas flock to the Ermita de San Antonio de la Florida on 13 June to petition for a partner.

Día de San Juan

Celebrated in other parts of Spain with fireworks and considerable gusto, the eve of this holiday (24 June) is a minor affair in Madrid. The action, such as it is, takes place in the Parque del Buen Retiro.

Día del Orgullo de Gays, Lesbianas y Transexuales

www.orgullogay.org, in Spanish
www.gaypridemadrid.com

The city's gay, lesbian and trans pride festival and parade takes place on the last Saturday of June. It's an international gig, with simultaneous parades taking places in cities across Europe, from Berlin to Paris. Chueca is the place to be.

JULY & AUGUST

Veranos de la Villa

www.esmadrid.com/veranosdelavilla
Throughout summer, the town authorities stage a series of exhibitions and concerts, opera, dance and theatre performances.

Known as 'Summers in the City', it takes over venues across the city from the Jardines de Sabatini to the Templo de Debod. The programme starts in July and runs to the end of August.

Fiestas de San Lorenzo, San Cayetano & La Virgen de la Paloma

These three local patron saints' festivities (which revolve around La Latina, Plaza de Lavapiés and Calle de Calatrava in La Latina respectively) keep the central districts of Madrid busy during the otherwise quiet first fortnight of August.

SEPTEMBER & OCTOBER

Local Fiestas

Several local councils organise fiestas in the first and second weeks of September, although these occasionally spill over into October. In the last week of the month you can check out the Fiesta de Otoño (Autumn Festival) in Chamartín in the far north of Madrid. These are all-singing, all-dancing affairs.

Fiesta de Otoño (Autumn Festival)

The city throws off the torpor of summer with a busy calendar of musical and theatrical activity right up to the approach to Christmas.

MADRID DIARY

Live jazz, Populart (p80)

NOVEMBER

Día de la Virgen de la Almudena
Castizos (true-blue Madrileños) gather in the Plaza Mayor to hear Mass on the feast day (9 November) of the city's female patron saint.

DECEMBER

Emociona Jazz
Madrid hosts a second jazz festival in December when groups from far and wide converge on the capital.

Festival de Gospel & Negro Spirituals
In the week running up to Christmas, Madrid is treated to a feast of jazz, blues and gospel, usually in the Centro Cultural de la Villa.

Navidad (Christmas)
This is a fairly quiet family time with the main meal on Christmas Eve *(Nochebuena)*. Elaborate nativity scenes (cribs) are set up in churches around the city and an exhibition of them is held in Plaza Mayor. *Feliz Navidad* (Happy Christmas)!

Outdoor cafés on Plaza de Santa Ana (p70)

ITINERARIES

With everything in Madrid just a short walk, quick Metro ride or cheap taxi journey from the centre, it's not surprising how much you can cram in if time is tight. An organised tour (p167) is one way to maximise your time. Following one of our itineraries is another.

DAY ONE

Plaza Mayor (p10) is a glorious place to get your bearings, while a coffee or glass of wine at an outdoor table on Plaza de Oriente (p14) is one of Madrid's more sedate but rewarding charms. The Museo del Prado (p12) is Madrid's standout highlight, while the souvenir hunters among you will gravitate towards El Arco Artesanía (p46) and Antigua Casa Talavera (p45). To taste the full spectrum of Madrid's culinary charms, eat lunch at Restaurante Sobrino de Botín (p51) and for dinner, cruise the tapas bars along Calle de la Cava Baja (p24). Finally, head for Huertas (p70) and get swept up in the night-time action.

DAY TWO

Head for the Centro de Arte Reina Sofía (p16) and Plaza de la Villa (p44). Try any of the restaurants along Calle de la Libertad in Chueca (p105) and pass the afternoon by taking an old-style bath and massage at Hammam Medina Mayrit (p57). A *mojito* (Cuban cocktail) at Delic (p67) on Plaza de la Paja gives you a front-row seat for the best of La Latina, while a meal of Galician tapas at Maceiras (p76) is the perfect preparation for Madrid's live-music smorgasbord – for flamenco head to Cardamomo (p80) or Las Carboneras (p55), for jazz try Café Central (p80). Finish your night at Museo Chicote (p112).

DAY THREE

After all the excitement of your first two days, have a lazy, artistic morning at the Museo Thyssen-Bornemisza (p84), pass by Plaza de la Cibeles (p85) then catch the Metro across town to the Ermita de San Antonio de la Florida (p46). After lunch at Casa Mingo (p46), consider a siesta then head for the Templo de Debod (p130). The old-world surrounds of Café

Top left Bear and strawberry tree (Madrid's symbol) push in front of King Carlos III on Plaza de la Puerta del Sol (p70) **Top right** Feel every shade of the sun above you in Lavapiés (p58) **Bottom** Wine, dine and look fine at cool La Musa (p121)

Comercial (p122) set you up nicely for a meal along Calle de Manuela Malasaña: La Musa (p121), La Isla del Tesoro (p120) or Nina (p121) should do the trick. If you've got energy to burn, immerse yourself in the night-life of Malasaña (p21) or Chueca (p18).

MADRILEÑO SUNDAY

Spend your Sunday morning at El Rastro (p11) before branching out into the bars of La Latina, especially along Calle de la Cava Baja (p24). Taberna Tempranillo (p69) is a barrio (neighbourhood) favourite, while tapas never tasted so good as at Txakolina (p66) or Casa Revuelta (p50). The ta-pas theme continues at Las Bravas (p76), and a vermouth at Casa Alberto (p75) is your ticket to honorary Madrileño status. After that, it just has to be the Parque del Buen Retiro (p17), where all Madrid comes out to play. As sunset approaches, listen for the drums…

SATURDAY NIGHT OUT

For an early evening drink, head for Café Belén (p108), El Jardín Secreto (p123), La Venencia (p78) or El Imperfecto (p78). If you like a casual

The goddess Cybele is the centrepiece at Plaza de la Cibeles (p85)

FORWARD PLANNING

Up to a month before you visit Madrid, make a booking at Sergi Arola Gastro (p132) and start perusing the local Spanish-language websites that give a rundown of upcoming concerts, exhibitions and other events. The better ones include Guía del Ocio (www.guiadelocio.com), La Netro (http://madrid.lanetro.com) and Salir.com (http://madrid.salir.com). If Spanish is a road too far, try the Madrid page of www.whatsonwhen.com, In Madrid (www.in-madrid .com) or the Madrid town hall's excellent multilingual website (www.esmadrid.com). Also worth checking out is Le Cool (http://lecool.com/madrid) which requires free registration but always has cutting-edge listings for upcoming events. Also check out Café Central (www .cafecentralmadrid.com) to see what headline jazz acts are on its programme.

For theatre performances, Real Madrid football games and bullfighting tickets, one recommended agency is Localidades Galicia (www.eol.es/lgalicia/). Tickets for football matches go on sale a week before the match. A week before you arrive, you can also make a reservation at Hammam Medina Mayrit (www.medinamayrit.com).

crowd, Malasaña (p21) or Lavapiés (p67) is for you. In the latter, La Inquilina (p68), El Eucalipto (p67), and El Juglar (p69) make a great circuit. Chueca (p18) and Huertas (p22) are equally energetic and a touch more upmarket, but don't neglect La Latina where Calle de la Cava Baja (p24), Almendro 13 (p64) and Taberna Tempranillo (p69) are terrific. To dance until dawn, Cool (p56) has a name that says it all, while Teatro Joy Eslava (p57) and Kapital (p87) are Madrid classics.

MUSEUM-FREE MONDAY

With most museums closed on Monday, it's time to shop. Head for Calle de Serrano (p19) in Salamanca to find the latest Spanish designers. To break things up, snack on the best *pintxos* (Basque tapas) at Biotza (p96) then get your fill of international brand-names along the exclusive Calle de José Ortega y Gasset (p95). Lunch at Sula (p100) is very Salamanca. Head for the boutiques of Calle de Piamonte (p104) in Chueca, then stop for sustenance at Maison Blanche (p107). Brazilian beats at Kabokla (p123) or live music at Clamores (p133) are mellow ways to round out your day.

>BARRIOS

Come outdoors, Plaza de Chueca

BARRIOS

Perhaps alone among the great cities of Europe, Madrid has a discernible centre encircled by barrios (neighbourhoods), each of which has its own personality.

Madrid is centred on the Plaza de la Puerta del Sol and Los Austrias, the city's oldest quarter. If your time is limited and your interest lies in catching an overall flavour of the city, this is probably where you'll spend the most time.

Away to the southwest lies La Latina, another old Madrid barrio with medieval streetscapes, fantastic bars and quirky shops. Down the hill to the south of the centre is gritty Lavapiés, which is off the well-trodden tourist trail, traditional and defiantly multicultural.

Huertas, immediately southeast of the centre, is perhaps the inner-city barrio that most lives for the night. Wonderful bars, clamorous night-time streets and an intriguing array of places to eat are hallmarks of Huertas, as are cosy venues for live jazz or flamenco. At the bottom of the Huertas hill, southeast across the Plaza del Emperador Carlos V, is Atocha, home to Madrid's biggest railway station.

By the time you reach the lower end of Huertas, you're close to the stately Paseo del Prado, which runs past Madrid's best art galleries. Up the hill to the east is the expansive Parque del Buen Retiro, which fronts onto Salamanca, Madrid's most exclusive and upmarket barrio. Salamanca is a shopper's paradise, with terrific restaurants to help provide sustenance while you shop. West of Salamanca, across the Paseo de los Recoletos, lies Chueca, the proudly gay barrio that has become a byword for a stylish, living-for-the-moment lifestyle that's hard to resist. Chueca's narrow lanes play host to some of the best restaurants and nightlife in Madrid. The neighbouring barrio of Malasaña (and its extension, Conde Duque) has a character all its own, sometimes stuck in a slightly down-at-heel 1970s time warp, but just as often being the place to find the coolest new restaurants, bars and shops. North of Chueca and Malasaña lie Chamberí and Argüelles, traditional Madrid barrios with wide, tree-lined streets; they're an easy Metro ride from the centre.

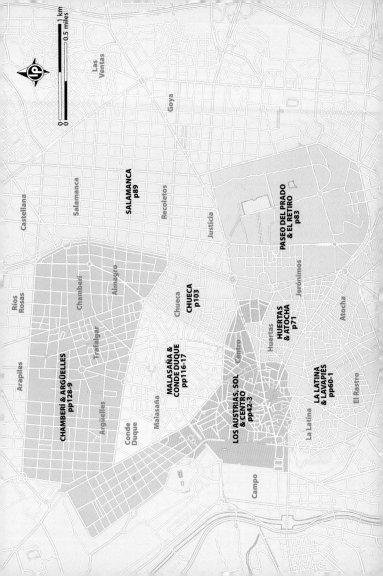

1 km
0.5 miles

Las Ventas

Goya

Salamanca

SALAMANCA
p89

Recoletos

Castellana

Justicia

PASEO DEL PRADO
& EL RETIRO
p83

Ríos Rosas

Chamberí

Almagro

Chueca

CHUECA
p103

Jerónimos

Trafalgar

CHAMBERÍ & ARGÜELLES
pp128-9

MALASAÑA &
CONDE DUQUE
pp116-17

Huertas

HUERTAS
& ATOCHA
p71

Arapiles

Malasaña

Centro

Atocha

Arguelles

Conde Duque

LOS AUSTRIAS,
SOL
& CENTRO
pp42-3

LA LATINA
& LAVAPIÉS
pp60-1

El Rastro

La Latina

Campo

>LOS AUSTRIAS, SOL & CENTRO

The heart of Madrid is where the Madrileño world most often intersects with that of tourists and expats drawn to that feel-good Madrid vibe. It's also a place to take the pulse of the city, for this is where the Madrid of old meets Spain's most prosperous modern city. From the quiet lanes of the old town to the great thoroughfares of the city, where people come to shop, eat and party, downtown Madrid has something for everyone.

The Plaza de la Puerta del Sol is Madrid's most important crossroad. From here, Calle Mayor and Calle del Arenal fan out west towards Madrid's most beautiful squares, home to much of Madrid life. West of the Plaza Mayor is Madrid's oldest corner, an area known as Madrid de los Austrias, in reference to the Habsburg dynasty that ruled Spain from 1517 to 1700.

LOS AUSTRIAS, SOL & CENTRO

Please see over for map

Calle de la Montera is the seedy end of central Madrid. A far better alternative is Calle de Preciados, which heads north towards the busy boulevard of Gran Vía.

◉ SEE

◉ CATEDRAL DE NUESTRA SEÑORA DE LA ALMUDENA

☎ 91 542 22 00; Calle de Bailén; cathedral donation €1, museum adult/child €6/4; 🕙 cathedral 9am-9pm, museum 10am-2.30pm Mon-Sat; Ⓜ Ópera; ♿
Madrid's cathedral is in perfect architectural harmony with the adjacent Palacio Real and this is where the appeal lies. The cathedral's museum allows you to climb to the dome with fine Madrid views.

◉ CONVENTO DE LAS DESCALZAS REALES

☎ 91 454 88 00; www.patrimonionacion al.es, in Spanish; Plaza de las Descalzas 3; adult/student & EU senior €5/2.50, EU citizens free Wed, combined ticket with Convento de la Encarnación €6/3.40; 🕙 10.30am-12.45pm & 4-5.45pm Tue-Thu & Sat, 10.30am-12.45pm Fri, 11am-1.45pm Sun & holidays; Ⓜ Callao or Ópera
Behind the sober plateresque façade of this 'Convent of the Barefooted Royals' lies a sumptuous stronghold of Catholic extravagance. The compulsory guided tour leads up a gaudily frescoed Renaissance stairway, past the convent's 33 chapels and, in the former sleeping quarters, some lavish tapestries.

◉ GRAN VÍA

Ⓜ Plaza de España, Gran Vía or Callao
One of Madrid's signature boulevards, Gran Vía was bulldozed through central Madrid in 1911 in a muscular, if ultimately successful example of town planning. Dominating the skyline is the 1920s-era Telefónica building, while the boulevard's southeastern end boasts the most spectacular façades, none more so than the stunning, French-designed Edificio Metrópolis (1905).

◉ PALACIO REAL

☎ 91 454 88 00; www.patrimonionacion al.es, in Spanish; Calle de Bailén; adult/student, child & EU señor €10/3.50, adult without guide €8, EU citizens free Wed, Armería Real €3.40/1.70; 🕙 9am-6pm Mon-Sat, 9am-3pm Sun & holidays Apr-Sep, 9.30am-5pm Mon-Sat, 9am-2pm Sun & holidays Oct-Mar; Ⓜ Ópera; ♿
Madrid's Royal Palace has been the headquarters for Spain's Bourbon dynasty for centuries and the lavish rooms that are open to the public are monuments to royal excess. For more information, see p14.

◉ PLAZA DE LA PUERTA DEL SOL

Ⓜ Sol; ♿
In Madrid's earliest days, the Puerta del Sol was the eastern

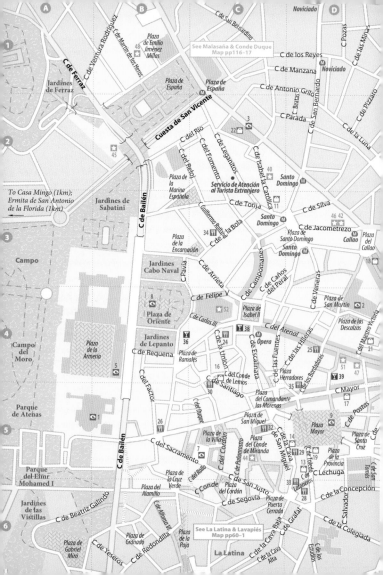

gate of the city, but Spain's Kilometre Zero is now a gracious hemisphere of elegant façades and overwhelming crowds. On New Year's Eve, people throng the square to bring in the New Year.

ⓒ PLAZA DE LA VILLA
Calle Mayor; guided tour of Ayuntamiento 5pm Mon free; Ⓜ **Ópera;** ♿
This intimate little square is dominated by the sober brick-and-slate architecture known as *barroco madrileño* (Madrid baroque). The permanent seat of Madrid's city government since the Middle Ages, it's still home to the Ayuntamiento (town hall), as well as the 15th-century Casa de los Lujanes, with its Gothic and Mudéjar touches, and the 16th-century Casa de Cisneros, which is now home to the Salón de Tapices (Tapestries Hall), adorned with exquisite 15th-century Flemish tapestries. It is visited as part of the Ayuntamiento tour.

ⓒ PLAZA DE ORIENTE
Ⓜ **Ópera;** ♿
The majestic Plaza de Oriente is one of the most elegant architectural arcs in all Madrid. Overlooked by the Palacio Real and Teatro Real, awash with marble statues and greenery and home to refined cafés, this is Madrid at its best. See p14 for more details.

ⓒ PLAZA MAYOR
Ⓜ **Sol;** ♿
If you had to choose just one image that was unmistakably Madrid, the Plaza Mayor would most likely be it. To see its epic history told in pictures, check out the carvings on the circular seats beneath the lampposts. See p10 for extended coverage.

ⓒ REAL ACADEMIA DE BELLAS ARTES DE SAN FERNANDO
☎ **91 524 08 64; http://rabasf.insde .es, in Spanish; Calle de Alcalá 13; adult/student/senior & under 18 yr**

HEADS UP

The Plaza Mayor's history is not all about bullfighting and the other grand passions of Madrid life. In 1673, King Carlos II issued an edict allowing the vendors to raise tarpaulins above their stalls to protect their wares and themselves from the refuse and raw sewage that people habitually tossed out of the windows above!

Madrileños can also be an irreverent bunch. In the middle of the present-day square stands an equestrian statue of the man who ordered its construction, Felipe III. Originally placed in the Casa de Campo, it was moved to the Plaza Mayor in 1848, whereafter it became a favoured meeting place for locals who frequently arrange to meet 'under the balls of the horse'.

Put yourself in the quintessential picture of Madrid at the Plaza Mayor

€3/1.50/free, free to all on Wed; ⏱ 9am-5pm Tue-Sat, 9am-2.30pm Sun Sep-Jun, varied hours in summer, guided tours 11am Tue, Thu & Fri; Ⓜ Sevilla This fascinating journey into another age of art encompasses masterpieces from Zurbarán, El Greco, José de Ribera, Velázquez, Rubens, Tintoretto and Goya. If the hoary old masters aren't your style, try upstairs where you'll find drawings by Picasso (who once studied here), as well as works by Sorolla, Juan Gris, Eduardo Chillida and Ignacio Zuloaga.

🛍 SHOP

Souvenirs dominate the downtown Madrid shopping picture, and amid the kitsch and bullfighting-posters-with-your-name-on-it are a number of outstanding smaller shops if you know where to look. Calle de Preciados is undoubtedly one of the premier shopping streets in Madrid, although it's more big stores than creative boutiques.

🏛 ANTIGUA CASA TALAVERA
Ceramics

☎ 91 547 34 17; Calle de Isabel la Católica 2; ⏱ 10am-1.30pm & 5-8pm Mon-Fri, 10am-1.30pm Sat; Ⓜ Santo Domingo They just don't make shops like this any more. The tiled façade conceals an Aladdin's cave of ceramics that come from small family potters all over Spain. Pieces range from the decorative (tiles) to the useful (plates, jugs and other kitchen items). The old couple who run the place are delightful.

BARRIOS

LOS AUSTRIAS, SOL & CENTRO

WORTH THE TRIP

Extraordinary frescoes by Goya adorn the ceiling of the otherwise modest **Ermita de San Antonio de la Florida** (☎ 91 542 07 22; Glorieta de San Antonio de la Florida 5; admission free; 🕑 9.30am-8pm Tue-Fri, 10am-2pm Sat & Sun, hours vary Jul & Aug; Ⓜ Príncipe Pío). Recently restored and also known as the Panteón de Goya, this is one of the few places to see Goya's work in its original setting. The painter is buried in front of the altar. The frescoes on the dome date from 1798 and depict the miracle of St Anthony, who miraculously appeared at the trial of his father, who was unjustly accused of murder. Anthony brought the corpse back to life and the corpse duly absolved his father.

If you're in the area, consider eating at **Casa Mingo** (☎ 91 547 79 18; Paseo de la Florida 34; 🕑 11am-midnight; Ⓜ Príncipe Pío), a rambling Asturian cider house that's known by just about every Madrileño, most of whom agree that there's no finer place to order *pollo asado* (roast chicken) and a bottle of cider.

To reach both the Ermita de San Antonio de la Florida and Casa Mingo, walk northwest along Paseo de la Florida from the Príncipe Pío Metro station. Casa Mingo is 600m along on your right and the Ermita is next door (the first of the two churches you'll see).

🗀 CASA DE DIEGO
Accessories

☎ 91 522 66 43; www.casadediego.com; Plaza de la Puerta del Sol 12; 🕑 9.30am-8pm Mon-Sat; Ⓜ Sol

The Spanish art of the *abanico* (fan) has no finer home than this landmark old shop right on the Plaza de la Puerta del Sol. The owners know their stuff, having sold and repaired Spanish fans, shawls, umbrellas and canes since 1858. Service is old-style and occasionally grumpy.

🗀 CASA HERNANZ *Shoes*

☎ 91 366 54 50; Calle de Toledo 18; 🕑 9am-1.30pm & 4.30-8pm Mon-Fri, 10am-2pm Sat; Ⓜ La Latina or Sol

The comfy, rope-soled *alpargatas* (espadrilles), Spain's traditional footwear, are worn by everyone from the King of Spain to the Pope and you can buy your own pair at this humble workshop and even get them especially made to order.

🗀 EL ARCO ARTESANÍA
Souvenirs

☎ 91 365 26 80; www.elarcoartesania .com; Plaza Mayor 9; 🕑 11am-9pm; Ⓜ Sol or La Latina

Central Madrid is awash with souvenirs but this store stands out from the crowd with stylish, designer souvenirs in the south-western corner of Plaza Mayor. Highlights include stone and glass-work, jewellery, home fittings and gorgeous papier-mâché figures.

🏛 EL CORTE INGLÉS
*Department Store &
Convenience Store*
☎ 91 379 80 00; www.elcorteingles.es;
Calle de Preciados 3; 🕙 10am-10pm Mon-
Sat, 11am-9pm Sun & holidays; Ⓜ Sol
Spain's largest department store
has everything you need and
many things you don't. It's standard department-store stuff, but
it has a broad range of Spanish
products and it's always handy to
know where it is.

🏛 EL FLAMENCO VIVE *Music*
☎ 91 547 39 17; www.elflamencovive
.com; Calle del Conde de Lemos 7;
🕙 10.30am-2pm & 5-9pm Mon-Sat;
Ⓜ Ópera
If you've fallen in love with flamenco, you'll fall in love with this small
temple to the art. Crowded inside
are guitars, songbooks, super-
cheap CDs, polka-dotted dancing
costumes, shoes, colourful plastic
jewellery and literature about
flamenco.

Precious treasures wait on Calle de Preciados

BARRIOS

LOS AUSTRIAS, SOL & CENTRO

🏠 FLIP
Fashion, Clothes & Accessories
☎ 91 366 44 72; Calle Mayor 19;
🕑 10.30am-9pm Mon-Sat; Ⓜ Sol
Too cool for its own good, Flip is
funky and edgy with its designer
T-shirts and G-Star jeans, a groovy
and often offbeat collection of
belts, caps and bags and staff that
will let you know how it all looks
and fits.

🏠 FNAC *Books & Music*
☎ 91 595 61 00; www.fnac.es; Calle de
Preciados 28; 🕑 10am-9.30pm Mon-Sat,
noon-9.30pm Sun; Ⓜ Callao
This four-storey megastore has
a terrific range of CDs, DVDs,
electronics and books; English-
language books are available on
the 3rd floor.

🏠 FORTUNATA – LA TIENDA
DE MADRID *Souvenirs*
☎ 91 364 16 82; www.latiendade
madrid.com; Calle de Toledo 3;
🕑 11am-2.30pm & 5-8.30pm Tue-Sat,
11am-2.30pm Sun; Ⓜ Sol
For quality Spanish souvenirs and
books about Madrid (mostly in
Spanish), Fortunata is a cut above
most souvenir shops in the city
centre. There's very little of the
mass-produced tourist kitsch on
offer here but there's plenty to
turn your head, including posters,
paper decorations and books.

🏠 JOSÉ RAMÍREZ *Music*
☎ 91 531 42 29; www.guitarrasramirez
.com; Calle de la Paz 8; 🕑 10am-2pm, 4.30-
8pm Mon-Fri, 10.30am-2pm Sat; Ⓜ Sol
As one of Spain's most accom-
plished guitar makers, José Ramí-
rez is one of the unsung heroes
of Spanish music. Everyone from
flamenco greats to the Beatles
have come here, and out the back
is a little museum with guitars dating back to 1830.

🏠 MATY *Flamenco Clothing*
☎ 91 531 32 91; www.maty.es, in
Spanish; Calle del Maestro Victoria 2;
🕑 10am-1.45pm & 4.30-8pm Mon-Fri,
10am-2pm & 4.30-8pm Sat; Ⓜ Sol
Unlike the not-so-cheap imitations
sold in souvenir stores across
the capital, Maty sells genuine
flamenco dresses, shoes and
accessories with sizes for children
and adults. These are the real deal,
with prices to match, but they
make brilliant gifts.

🏠 SALVADOR BACHILLER
Fashion & Accessories
☎ 91 559 83 21; www.salvadorbachiller
.com; Gran Vía 65; 🕑 10am-9.30pm
Mon-Sat; Ⓜ Plaza de España or Santo
Domingo
Spanish women (and quite a
few men) love Salvador Bachiller
and it's not hard to see why. It's
all about quality leather, bright
colours and an extensive array of

bags, wallets, shoes, suitcases and other accessories.

🍴 EAT

The restaurants of central Madrid reflect the fact that this is a catch-all barrio (neighbourhood) where many personalities converge rather than having one easily defined character. Although there are exceptions to the rule, the cooler, designer restaurants are either close to the eastern end of Gran Vía or north of Plaza de Isabel II, while more traditional offerings are to be found closer to Plaza Mayor.

🍴 AL NATURAL Vegetarian   €€
☎ 91 369 47 09; www.alnatural.biz; Calle de Zorrilla 11; ⏱ 1-4pm & 8.30pm-midnight Mon-Sat, 1-4pm Sun; Ⓜ Sevilla or Banco de España; ♿ Ⓥ ♿
Tucked away behind the Spanish parliament, Al Natural has an intimate ambience and terrific vegetarian food. There are the usual suspects such as salads and pastas, but some welcome creative touches, including grilled provolone cheeses, make this a terrific choice.

🍴 ALGARABÍA La Rioja   €€
☎ 91 542 41 31; Calle de la Unión 8; ⏱ 2-4.30pm & 9.30pm-midnight Mon-Fri, 9.30pm-midnight Sat; Ⓜ Ópera; ♿
You know the wines of La Rioja, but the food of this northern Spanish region is also filled with flavour. The

> ### THE ORIGIN OF TAPAS
> As traders, pilgrims and journeymen headed to the capital or elsewhere, they holed up in inns where innkeepers, concerned about drunken men on horseback setting out from their village, developed a tradition of putting a 'lid' (tapa) of bread with a small piece of meat or cheese atop a glass of wine or beer. It was partly to keep the bugs out, but primarily to encourage people not to drink on an empty stomach. Thus it was that tapas became an essential part of the Spanish eating experience.

cuisine here is all about home-cooking and choosing the menú de degustación is a great way to get an overview of the regional specialties. The croquetas (croquettes) have a loyal following and, not surprisingly, the wine list is excellent.

🍴 BANGKOK THAI RESTAURANT Thai   €
☎ 91 559 16 96; 1st fl, Calle de los Bordadores 15; ⏱ 12.30-4pm & 8pm-midnight; Ⓜ Sol or Ópera; ♿
Delicious Thai food, reasonable prices (the menú del día – menu of the day – goes for €11.50), good service and a subtly stylish dining area make for a terrific meal in the heart of town. If you're lucky, you'll get one of the tables overlooking the busy street life of Calle de Arenal. Unusually for Madrid, it's a nonsmoking restaurant.

BARRIOS

LOS AUSTRIAS, SOL & CENTRO

🍴 CASA CIRIACO
Spanish   €€

☎ 91 548 06 20; Calle Mayor 84; ⏰ 1-4pm & 8pm-midnight Thu-Tue, closed Aug; Ⓜ Ópera; ♿ ☕

One of the *grande dames* of the Madrid restaurant scene, Casa Ciriaco has witnessed attempted assassinations (of King Alfonso XIII in 1906) and was immortalised by the Spanish writer Valle-Inclán who set part of his novel *Luces de Bohemia* here. Its legend made, it now puts all its energies into fine Madrileño cooking from seafood to hearty meat dishes.

🍴 CASA LABRA
Tapas   €€

☎ 91 531 00 81; Calle de Tetuán 12; ⏰ 11am-3.30pm & 6-11pm; Ⓜ Sol; ♿

Going strong since 1860, Casa Labra is one of the most emblematic old *tabernas* (taverns) of Madrid. It's famous for its *bacalao* (cod) but there's so much history and character attached to the place as well.

🍴 CASA REVUELTA
Tapas   €

☎ 91 366 33 32; Calle de Latoneros 3; ⏰ 10am-4pm & 7-11pm Tue-Sat, 10am-4pm Sun; Ⓜ Sol or La Latina

While aficionados of Casa Labra may disagree, Casa Revuelta wins our prize for Madrid's finest tapas of *bacalao* (cod). The fact that the old owner painstakingly extracts

> ## A BAR WITH HISTORY
> Casa Labra has taken on an almost mythical status in the history of Madrid, for it was here, in 1879, clandestinely, in a small back room, that the Partido Socialista Obrero Español (PSOE; Spanish Socialist Party), which now rules Spain, was founded. Later, Pío Baroja immortalised the bar in his novel *La Busca*. Despite its left-wing origins, it was one of the few bars to survive Franco's remodelling of the bars that once encircled the Plaza de la Puerta del Sol. Having thus taken on the quality of a legend, it's the sort of place where fathers bring their sons, as their fathers did before them, in what has become a rite of Madrileño passage.

every fish-bone in the morning wins the argument for us. Early on a Sunday afternoon, as the Rastro crowd gathers in this virtually hidden bar, it's filled to the rafters with that inexplicable feel-good Madrid buzz.

🍴 KITCHEN STORIES
Spanish Fusion   €€

☎ 91 366 97 71; www.kitchenstories.es, in Spanish; Calle de los Cuchilleros 3; ⏰ 11.30am-1am; Ⓜ Sol or La Latina

Café, restaurant and food store in one, Kitchen Stories, at the foot of the Arco de Cuchilleros stairs, is a copy of similar places springing up across the city with Spanish and fusion dishes.

🍴 LA GASTROTECA DE SANTIAGO
Spanish Fusion €€

☎ 91 548 07 07; www.lagastroteca desantiago.es; Plaza de Santiago 1; ⏱ 2-4pm & 9pm-midnight; Ⓜ Sol or Ópera

Indulge the gastronome in you. The home kitchen of the Córdoba-born chef Juan Carlos Ramos, La Gastroteca de Santiago deploys the freshest ingredients in homage to the finest in traditional Spanish cooking, with experimental twists and international influences along the way – an exemplary combination that rarely misses a beat. A 250-strong wine list, designer space and large servings make this a special choice.

🍴 LA GLORIA DE MONTERA
Fusion €€€

☎ 91 523 44 07; Calle del Caballero de Gracia 10; ⏱ 1.15-4pm & 8.30-11.45pm; Ⓜ Gran Vía

Part of a welcome Madrid trend towards stylish designer décor, creative cooking and extremely reasonable prices, La Gloria de Montera is one of the best places to enjoy a sophisticated meal in downtown Madrid. Dishes such as fish tempura (€7.45) are typical of the international flavours given a Spanish twist. It doesn't take reservations.

🍴 MERCADO DE SAN MIGUEL
Delicatessen €€

www.mercadodesanmiguel.es, in Spanish; Plaza de San Miguel; ⏱ 10am-10pm Sun-Wed, 10am-2am Thu-Sat; Ⓜ Sol

One of Madrid's oldest and most beautiful markets, the Mercado de San Miguel has recently undergone a major renovation and bills itself as a 'culinary cultural centre'. Within the early 20th-century glass walls, the market has become an inviting space strewn with tables where you can enjoy the freshest food or a drink.

🍴 RESTAURANTE SOBRINO DE BOTÍN *Spanish* €€

☎ 91 366 42 17; www.botin.es; Calle de los Cuchilleros 17; ⏱ 1-4pm & 8pm-midnight; Ⓜ La Latina or Sol; ♿

The world's oldest restaurant (1725), Restaurante Sobrino de Botín appeared in Hemingway's *The Sun Also Rises* and has more than a whiff of legend about it. The secret of its longevity is fine *cochinillo* (suckling pig) and *cordero asado* (roast lamb) cooked in the wood-fired ovens and served in the vaulted cellar. Service is good, if a little too rapid.

🍴 TABERNA LA BOLA
Traditional Spanish €€

☎ 91 547 69 30; www.labola.es; Calle de la Bola 5; ⏱ 1-4pm & 8.30-11pm, Mon-Sat, 1-4pm Sun; Ⓜ Santo Domingo

In polls for the most traditional Madrid cuisine, Taberna La Bola (open since 1870) always features near the top. If you're going to try *cocido a la Madrileña* (chickpea stew with soup and meat, €19), this is a good place to do so. It serves other Madrid specialities, including *callos* (tripe) and *sopa de ajo* (garlic soup).

🍴 YERBABUENA
Vegetarian €€

☎ 91 548 08 11; www.yerbabuena .ws; Calle de Bordadores 3; ⏰ 11.30am-midnight; Ⓜ Sol or Ópera; ♿ Ⓥ ♿

Cheerful bright colours, a full range of vegetarian staples (vegetable sausages, soy-bean hamburgers, biological rice and homemade yoghurt) and plenty of creatively conceived salads add up to one of central Madrid's best restaurants for vegetarians.

🍸 DRINK

Many of the tapas bars listed under 'Eat' also make great places to drink. Otherwise, you're more likely to find bars with more character in the neighbouring barrios of La Latina, Huertas, Malasaña or Chueca. Cafés are, however, something of a speciality of the plazas in the centre of town.

🍸 CAFÉ DE ORIENTE *Café*

☎ 91 541 39 74; Plaza de Oriente 2; ⏰ 8.30am-1.30am Mon-Thu, 9am-2.30am Fri & Sat, 9am-1.30am Sun; Ⓜ Ópera; ♿ ♿

Located strategically on one of Madrid's prettiest squares, in what was once part of a long-disappeared, 17th-century convent, the place feels like a set out of central Europe. It's the perfect spot for a coffee (or good

---

MENÚ DEL DÍA

One great way to save money while eating well is the *menú del día*, which is, by law, available at every Spanish restaurant, at lunchtime from Monday to Friday. The *menú del día* is a set-price meal of the day that comprises three courses, with bread and a drink (usually wine and water but coffee is extra) thrown in. You'll be given a menu with five or six starters, the same number of mains and a handful of desserts – choose one from each category and don't even think of mixing and matching. You can often find them for around €9 to €12.

Although the traveller's friend, the *menú del día* is aimed mainly at locals. Lunchtime is the main meal of the Madrid day, and during the working week few Madrileños have time to go home for lunch. Taking a packed lunch is just not the done thing, so most end up eating in restaurants – all-inclusive three-course meals are as close as they can come to eating home-style food without breaking the bank.

wine) and paper, especially on the *terraza (terrace)* when the weather's fine.

▼ CAFÉ DEL CÍRCULO DE BELLAS ARTES *Café*
☎ 91 521 69 42; Calle de Alcalá 42; ☾ 9.45am-1am; Ⓜ Sevilla
This wonderful *belle époque* café was designed by Antonio Palacios in 1919 and boasts chandeliers and the charm of a bygone era. You have to buy a temporary club membership (€1) to drink here, except between 2pm and 4pm, but it's worth it; the service is a little stuffy.

▼ CAFÉ DEL REAL *Café*
☎ 91 547 21 24; Plaza de Isabel II 2; ☾ 9am-12.30am Sun-Thu, 9am-2.30am Fri & Sat; Ⓜ Ópera; ♿
Whether you long for a creative coffee or something a little stronger, Café del Real is one of our favourites. The low ceilings, wooden beams and leather chairs upstairs are a great place to pass an afternoon with friends as the lounge music keeps the atmosphere chilled.

▼ CHOCOLATERÍA DE SAN GINÉS *Café*
☎ 91 365 65 46; Pasadizo de San Ginés 5; ☾ 9.30am-7am Mon-Fri, 9am-7am Sat & Sun; Ⓜ Sol; ♿ 🚻

Perhaps the best known of Madrid's *chocolate con churros* (doughnut strips with chocolate) vendors, this Madrid institution is at its most popular from 3am to 6am as clubbers make a last stop for sustenance on their way home. Only in Madrid.

⭐ PLAY
The larger nightclubs of central Madrid are some of the most popular in Madrid especially for the international crowd (not surprising given their location). We're not saying that these are the best you'll find in town, but they're enough to satisfy all but the most discerning visitors. Most of the city's larger theatres, flamenco venues and cinema complexes offering films in the original versions are also found here.

⭐ CINEMAS & THEATRES
✦ RENOIR *Cinema*
☎ 902 229 122; www.cinesrenoir.com, in Spanish; Calle de Princesa 3; Ⓜ Plaza de España or Ventura Rodríguez
One of the most popular *versión original* (original version with Spanish subtitles) cinemas in Madrid, Renoir hosts plenty of latest-release films but with some interesting documentaries and Asian flicks as well.

⭐ TEATRO DE LA ZARZUELA
Theatre

☎ 91 524 54 00; http://teatrodela
zarzuela.mcu.es; Calle de Jovellanos 4;
Ⓜ Banco de España

This 1856 theatre is the premier
place to see zarzuela, the often-
satirical theatre-opera combination that Madrid has made its own.
The theatre also hosts mainstream
shows, as well as a smattering of
classical music and opera. Tickets
range from €12 to €36.

⭐ TEATRO REAL
Opera

☎ 902 244 848; www.teatro-real.com;
Plaza de Oriente; Ⓜ Ópera

After spending €100 million-
plus on a rebuilding project, the
Teatro Real is as technologically
advanced as any venue in Europe,
and although it may lack the old-
world grandeur of the continent's
great opera houses, it does host
high-class operas and occasional
ballets.

Theatre and opera collide on stage in zarzuela at Teatro de la Zarzuela

⭐ YELMO CINEPLEX IDEAL
Cinema

☎ 91 369 25 18, 902 220922; www
.yelmocineplex.es; Calle del Doctor
Cortezo 6; Ⓜ Tirso de Molina; ♿
Handy if you fancy an original-
language film while meandering
around downtown Madrid, Yelmo
has a good mix of major films and
more offbeat offerings.

⭐ LIVE MUSIC

⭐ EL BERLÍN JAZZ CAFÉ *Jazz*

☎ 91 521 57 52; www.cafeberlin.es, in
Spanish; Calle de Jacometrezo 4; admission €6-12; ⏱ 7pm-2.30am Tue-Sun;
Ⓜ Callao or Santo Domingo
El Berlín is a Madrid jazz stalwart
and one of the best places in town
for authentic jazz. The atmosphere is vaguely cabaret and the
headline acts a who's who of
world jazz.

⭐ LAS CARBONERAS
Flamenco

☎ 91 542 86 77; www.tablaolascarbon
eras.com, in Spanish; Plaza del Conde de
Miranda 1; admission from €30; ⏱ 9pm
& 10.30pm Mon-Thu, 9pm & 11pm Fri &
Sat; Ⓜ Ópera, Sol or La Latina
Like most of the *tablaos* (restaurants with a flamenco floorshow)
around town, this place sees far
more tourists than locals, but the
quality is top-notch – one of the
few places that flamenco aficiona-

LA ZARZUELA

What began in the late 17th century as
a way to amuse King Felipe IV and his
court has become one of Spain's most
unique theatre styles. With a light-
hearted combination of music and
dance, and a focus on everyday people's
problems, zarzuelas quickly became
popular in Madrid, which remains the
genre's undoubted capital. Although
you'll likely have trouble following the
storyline (zarzuelas are notoriously full
of local references and jokes), seeing a
zarzuela gives an entertaining look into
local culture.

dos seem to have no complaints
about.

⭐ LAS TABLAS *Flamenco*

☎ 91 542 05 20; www.lastablasmadrid
.com, in Spanish; Plaza de España 9;
admission €24; ⏱ 10.30pm Sun-Thu, 8pm
& 10pm Fri & Sat; Ⓜ Plaza de España
One of the more recent newcom-
ers to Madrid's flamenco scene,
Las Tablas has quickly earned a
reputation for quality flamenco.
Antonia Moya, the principal
dancer, often dances with the
famous Sara Baras when she is
on tour.

⭐ SALA EL SOL *Live Music*

☎ 91 532 64 90; Calle de los Jardines 3;
admission €9; ⏱ 11pm-5.30am Tue-Sat;
Ⓜ Gran Vía or Sol

Madrid's nocturnal heart pounds 365 nights a year at Teatro Joy Eslava

Sala El Sol opened in 1979, just in time for *la movida madrileña* (sociocultural movement in the years after the death of Francisco Franco) and quickly established itself as a leading stage for the icons of the era. *La movida* lives on here, where the music rocks and rolls through the '70s and '80s.

Cool by name and cool by nature. One of the hottest clubs in the city, where the curvy white lines and the curvaceous clientele are a perfect fit. Discreet lounge chairs in corners and a pulsating dance floor are protected by a strict entry policy. Things don't get going until 3am.

⭐ NIGHTCLUBS

⭐ COOL *Nightclub*
☎ 902 499 994; Calle de Isabel la Católica 6; admission €10-15; 🕐 midnight-6am Thu-Sat; Ⓜ Santo Domingo

⭐ COSTELLO CAFÉ & NIGHTCLUB *Nightclub & Café*
www.costelloclub.com; Calle del Caballero de Gracia 10; admission free; 🕐 6pm-1am Sun-Wed, 6pm-2.30am Thu-Sat; Ⓜ Gran Vía

The wave of intimate, chic clubs sweeping Madrid can promise much, but the House music is usually the same in most places. Costello Café & Nightclub is an exception with smooth-as-silk surrounds wedded to an innovative mix of pop, rock and fusion in Warhol-esque surrounds.

⭐ OBA OBA *Nightclub*
Calle de Jacometrezo 4; 🕑 **11pm-5.30am;** Ⓜ **Callao**
This nightclub is Brazilian down to its G-strings with live music some nights and dancing till dawn every night of the week. You'll find plenty of Brazilians in residence which is the best recommendation we can give for the music caipirinhas.

⭐ PALACIO GAVIRIA
Nightclub
☎ **91 526 60 69; www.palaciogaviria .com; Calle del Arenal 9; admission €10-15;** 🕑 **11pm-4am Mon-Wed, 10.30pm-5.30am Thu-Sat, 8.30pm-2am Sun;** Ⓜ **Sol**
An elegant palace converted into one of the most popular dance clubs in Madrid, Palacio Gaviria draws a mixed local and international crowd with music that's not too challenging but is designed to get you dancing. The crowd can

be pretty young and boisterous and the queues are sometimes long.

⭐ TEATRO JOY ESLAVA
Nightclub
☎ **91 366 37 33; www.joy-eslava.com, in Spanish; Calle del Arenal 11; admission Sun-Thu €12, Fri & Sat €15;** 🕑 **11.30pm-6am Sun-Thu, 6-10.15pm & 11.30pm-6am Fri & Sat;** Ⓜ **Sol**
The only things guaranteed at this grand Madrid dance club (housed in a 19th-century theatre) are a crowd and the fact that they'll be open (they claim to have opened every single day for the past 25 years). Expect the occasional *famoso* (celebrity) and recognisable international dance tunes.

⭐ SPAS
⭐ HAMMAM MEDINA MAYRIT
Spa
☎ **902 333 334; www.medinamayrit .com; Calle de Atocha 14;** 🕑 **10am-midnight;** Ⓜ **Sol**
Madrid's origins as a Muslim garrison town come alive at this wonderful old bathhouse. Set amid excavated cellars of old Madrid, it offers massages and aromatherapy beneath the elegantly restored arches. Reservations are required.

>LA LATINA & LAVAPIÉS

La Latina is one of Madrid's most happening barrios (neighbourhoods) with the one-time Moorish quarter of medieval Christian Madrid providing the backdrop for some of the city's best bars and restaurants. So many hubs of activity centre on Calle de la Cava Baja and the surrounding streets, while the climbing cobblestone streets between Calle de Segovia and Plaza de San Andrés are pretty by day and come alive at night. In this area, Plaza de la Paja is cosy and filled with charm. But the barrio is never busier than on Sunday when the Madrid institution of El Rastro flea market draws people from all across the city to the area where La Latina meets Lavapiés.

Lavapiés is at once Madrid's most traditional barrio and its most multicultural. It's quirky, alternative and a melting pot all in one and, despite the diversity, you get the rare sense of a community where everyone seems to know one another. Lavapiés life revolves around the Plaza de Lavapiés.

LA LATINA & LAVAPIÉS

Please see over for map

◉ SEE
◉ BASÍLICA DE NUESTRA SEÑORA DEL BUEN CONSEJO
☎ 91 369 20 37; Calle de Toledo 37;
🕑 8am-noon & 6-8.30pm; Ⓜ Tirso de Molina

This austere baroque basilica, also known as Catedral de San Isidro, served as Madrid's cathedral for centuries. Founded in the 17th century as the headquarters for the Jesuits, it now marks the final resting place of Madrid's patron saint, San Isidro.

◉ BASÍLICA DE SAN FRANCISCO EL GRANDE
☎ 91 365 38 00; Plaza de San Francisco; admission €3; 🕑 8-11am Mon, 8am-1pm & 4-6.30pm Tue-Fri, 4-8.45pm Sat; Ⓜ La Latina or Puerta de Toledo 🚌 3, 60 or 148; ♿

Legend has it that St Francis of Assisi built a chapel on this site in 1217. The imposing baroque basilica that you now see has an unusual floor plan, some wonderful frescoed cupolas and fine Renaissance-era walnut-sculpted seats where the church's superiors once met.

◉ IGLESIA DE SAN ANDRÉS
☎ 91 365 48 71; Plaza de San Andrés; 🕑 8am-1pm & 5.30-8pm; Ⓜ La Latina

One of the most important churches of old Madrid, the Iglesia

PEDRO ALMODÓVAR'S MADRID
> **Plaza Mayor** (p10) – *Flor de mi Secreto* (Flower of my Secret; 1995)
> **El Rastro** (p11) – *Laberinto de Pasiones* (Labyrinth of Passions; 1982)
> **Villa Rosa** (p81) – *Tacones Lejanos* (High Heels; 1991)
> **Café del Círculo de Bellas Artes** (p53) – *Kika* (1993)
> **Acueducto de Segovia** (Segovia Aqueduct; Calle de Bailén) – *Matador* (1986)
> **Museo del Jamón** (Calle Mayor 7, Centro) – *Carne Tremula* (Live Flesh; 1997)

de San Andrés is notable for its extraordinary baroque altar, columns flecked with gold leaf, and sculpted cherubic fantasies adorning the dome. The façade is at its best when illuminated by night as a backdrop for local café life.

◉ MUSEO DE SAN ISIDRO
☎ 91 366 74 15; www.munimadrid.es/museosanisidro; Plaza de San Andrés 2; admission free; 🕑 9.30am-8pm Tue-Fri, 10am-2pm Sat & Sun; Ⓜ La Latina

On the site where Madrid's patron saint, San Isidro Labrador (St Isidro, the farm labourer) ended his days around 1172, this small museum is dedicated to the saint's life. The highlight is a model based on Pedro Teixera's 1656 map of Madrid.

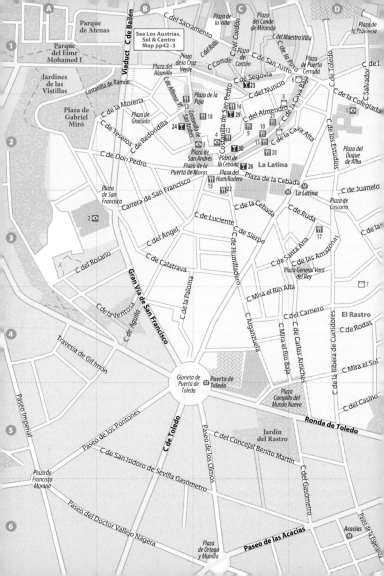

A

Parque
de Atenas

Parque
del Eimr
Mohamed I

Jardines
de las
Vistillas

Plaza de
Gabriel Miró

Plaza de San
Francisco

Carrera de San Francisco

Travesia de Gil Imón

Paseo Imperial

Plaza de
Francisco
Morano

B

Viaduct

C de Bailén

Costanilla de Ramón

C de la Morería

Plaza de
Granado

C de Yeseros

C de Redondilla

C de Don Pedro

Gran Vía de San Francisco

C de la Ventosa

C de Aguila

Paseo del Doctor Vallejo Nágera

See Los Austrias,
Sol & Centro
Map pp42-3

C del Sacramento

Plaza de la
Cruz Verde

Plaza del
Alamillo

C de Almendro

Plaza de la
Paja

13
18

24

Plaza de
San Andrés
Plaza de la
Puerta de Moros

3

C del Rosario

C del Angel

C de Calatrava

C de la Paloma

Paseo de los Pontones

C de San Isidoro de Sevilla

Glorieta de
Puerta de
Toledo

C de Toledo

Gasómetro

C

Plaza de
la Villa

C del Rollo

C de Conde

Plaza de la
Villa

Plaza del
Conde de
Miranda

C del Cordón

Plaza del
Cordón

C de San Justo

C de Segovia

C del Nuncio

Costanilla de San Pedro

Plaza de la
Cebada

30

26

Plaza del
Humilladero

15

C de Luciente

C de Sierpe

C de Humilladero

Plaza de la Cebada

C de la Cebada

C de Ruda

C de Santa Ana

C de las Amazonas

Plaza General Vara
del Rey

C Mira el Río Alta

C Argonzuela

C Mira el Río Baja

Puerta de
Toledo

Paseo de los Olmos

Jardín
del Rastro

C del Concejal Benito Martín

Plaza de
Ortega
y Munilla

D

Plaza de
la Província

C de Toledo

Plaza de
Puerta
Cerrada

C de la Colegiata

C de los Estudios

Plaza del
Duque
de Alba

C de Juanelo

La Latina

Plaza de
Cascorro

17

7

El Rastro

C de Rodas

C Mira el Sol

C de la Ribera de Curtidores

Plaza
Campillo del
Mundo Nuevo

Ronda de Toledo

C del Gasómetro

C del Casino

Acacias

Paseo de las Acacias

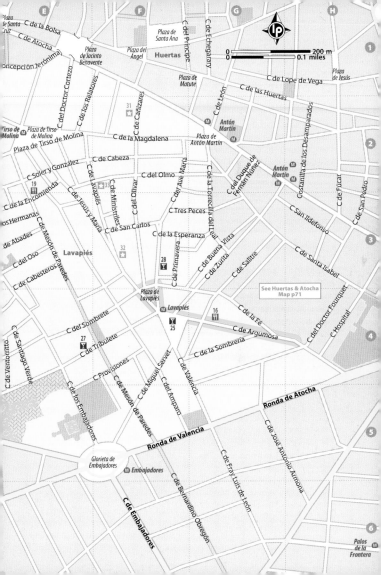

SHOP

Shopping in La Latina is all about stumbling upon charming but invariably small boutiques that manage to combine impeccable designer taste with quirky touches. Calle de la Cava Baja and the surrounding streets are where to start your search. Then, of course, there's El Rastro, the most atmospheric and diverse of all Madrid shopping experiences.

CARMEN SÁNCHEZ
Jewellery & Accessories

☎ 91 366 74 01; carmensanchezjoyas@hotmail.com; Calle de la Cava Baja 25; ⌚ noon-3pm & 7-10pm Tue-Sat, noon-4pm Sun; Ⓜ La Latina
This charming little boutique is typical of La Latina – sophisticated jewellery with the occasional quirky twist. Silver, enamel and beautiful colour combinations are the hallmark.

DEL HIERRO
Fashion & Accessories

☎ 91 364 58 91; Calle de la Cava Baja 6; ⌚ 11.30am-2.30pm & 5-9pm Mon-Sat, noon-3pm Sun; Ⓜ La Latina or Tirso de Molina
If you're looking for a handbag that captures the essence of chic modern Spain, this boutique has a small-but-exceptional selection from designers such as Iñaki

Sampedro, Quique Mestre and Carlos de Caz. The look is sophisticated, hand-painted and colourful.

EL RASTRO *Market*

Calle de la Ribera de Curtidores; ⌚ 8am-2pm Sun; Ⓜ La Latina, Puerta de Toledo or Tirso de Molina
Cheap clothes, luggage, antiques, old photos of Madrid, old flamenco records, grungy T-shirts, household goods and electronics are El Rastro staples, but for every 10 pieces of junk, there's a real gem waiting to be found. See p11 for more information.

HELENA ROHNER
Fashion & Jewellery

☎ 91 365 79 06; www.helenarohner .com; Calle de Almendro 4; ⌚ 9am-8.30pm Mon-Fri, noon-2.30pm & 3.30-8pm Sat, noon-3pm Sun; Ⓜ La Latina or Tirso de Molina
One of Europe's most creative jewellery designers, Rohner has a spacious, chic boutique that finds the perfect home in La Latina. Working with silver, stone and Murano glass, her work is inventive and a regular feature in Paris fashion shows.

EAT

For the most part, La Latina is all about the best tapas in Madrid, with a few traditional sit-down options thrown in for a bit of variety.

Giles Tremlett
Madrid correspondent for the Guardian *newspaper*

How long have you lived in Madrid? 17 years. **You must have seen some changes over the years. What stands out?** Thanks to immigration, Madrid has become a multiethnic city and is much more cosmopolitan as a result. **In which barrio do you live?** Retiro. **What is your favourite corner of Madrid?** The bars along Calle Doctor Castelo and the *terrazas* (outdoor tables) along Calle de Ibiza. Also the Parque del Buen Retiro, at least when the drums aren't playing… **What do you love most about living in Madrid?** Apart from the bars, I love the sensation of living in a barrio. I've lived around Retiro for the past 13 years and I love the barrio feel. Before that, I lived in the city centre where you don't get that same sense of barrio life. **What's special about Madrid?** It's such a great city for kids. Here they treat children like human beings, it's very safe and they can start to go out on their own much younger than they can in many other cities. **Madrid is…**Not Barcelona. It's also Old Spain trying to be New Spain.

Calle de la Cava Baja just might be the most rewarding tapas street in Madrid, while Plaza de la Paja also wins many hearts. In Lavapiés, there are dozens of low-budget international restaurants, as reflects the barrio itself, but Calle de Argumosa is the best place to eat.

🍴 ALMENDRO 13 *Tapas* €€
☎ 91 365 42 52; Calle de Almendro 13; 🕒 1-4pm & 7.30pm-12.30am Mon-Fri, 1-5pm & 8pm-1am Sat & Sun; Ⓜ La Latina
Regularly voted among the top 10 tapas bars in Madrid, Almendro 13 is a charming, wildly popular *taberna* (tavern) where you come for traditional Spanish tapas with an emphasis on quality rather than frilly elaborations.

🍴 CASA LUCAS *Tapas* €€
☎ 91 365 08 04; Calle de la Cava Baja 30; 🕒 1-3.30pm & 8pm-midnight Mon, Tue, Thu & Fri, 8pm-midnight Wed, 1-4pm & 8pm-1am Sat & Sun; Ⓜ La Latina
One of Madrid's best tapas bars, Casa Lucas is highly original and has been doing creative tapas long before they became fashionable. It's often packed to the rafters and we only ever hear praise about this place.

🍴 CASA LUCIO
Madrileño €€€
☎ 91 365 32 52; www.casalucio.es, in Spanish; Calle de la Cava Baja 35;

🕒 1-4pm & 9pm-midnight Sun-Fri, 9pm-midnight Sat Sep-Jul, closed Aug; Ⓜ La Latina
The king of Spain is among the many admirers of this old-style temple to gastronomy. The secret is a light touch, quality ingredients and traditional local cooking (think seafood, roasted meats and eggs). There's also *rabo de toro* (bull's tail) during the bullfighting season and plenty of Rioja wine to wash away the mere thought of it.

🍴 CORAZON LOCO *Tapas* €€
☎ 91 366 57 83; Calle del Almendro 22; 🕒 7pm-1.30am Mon-Wed, 12.30pm-1.30am Thu & Sun, 12.30pm-2.30am Fri & Sat; Ⓜ La Latina
In a barrio replete with tapas options, it takes something pretty special to catch our eye. Corazon Loco (Crazy Heart) is a splendid little tapas bar blending subtle tastes with a regularly changing menu and cheap wines.

🍴 EL ESTRAGÓN
Vegetarian €€
☎ 91 365 89 82; Plaza de la Paja 10; 🕒 1.30-4.30pm & 8pm-12.30am; Ⓜ La Latina; Ⓥ
A delightful spot for crepes, veggie burgers and other vegetarian specialities, El Estragón is undoubtedly one of Madrid's best vegetarian restaurants. Attentive vegans won't appreciate the use of butter.

ENE RESTAURANTE
Fusion €€

☎ 91 366 25 91; www.enerestaurante
.com; Calle del Nuncio 19; ⏱ 1.30pm-
2.30am Mon-Thu, 12.30pm-3.30am
Fri-Sun; Ⓜ La Latina

Ene is cool in all the right places
with a red-and-purple colour
scheme, helpful service, lounge
music, chill-out beds from which
to eat (there are also tables) and
a varied menu that includes
à la carte or tapas. The only
complaint? The brunch is a little
expensive for what you get.

JUANALALOCA
Tapas €€

☎ 91 364 05 25; Plaza de la Puerta de Moros 4; ⏱ 1.30-5.30pm & 8.30pm-12.30am
Tue-Fri, 1pm-1am Sat & Sun, 8.30pm-
12.30am Mon; Ⓜ La Latina; ♿ ♿

You can't miss 'Juana the Crazy
One' with its bright purple façade,
and nor would you want to.
With the finest *tortilla de patatas*
(potato omelette) in Madrid and
a feel-good buzz, especially in the
evening, it's one of the best places
to hang out in La Latina.

LA BUGA DEL LOBO
Spanish €€

☎ 91 467 61 51; www.labocadellobo
.com, in Spanish; Calle de Argumosa 11;
⏱ 11am-2am Wed-Mon; Ⓜ Lavapiés

La Buga del Lobo has been one of
the 'in' places in Lavapiés for years

now. The atmosphere is bohemian
and inclusive with funky, swirling
murals, contemporary art exhibitions and jazz or lounge music.
Conversely, the food is good and
traditional.

MALACATÍN *Madrileño* €€

☎ 91 365 52 41; Calle de Ruda 5;
⏱ 11am-5pm, 8-11pm Mon-Fri, 11am-
5pm Sat Sep-July; Ⓜ La Latina

If you want to see discerning
Madrileños enjoying their favourite
local food, this is arguably the
best place to do so. The clamour
of conversation – an essential part
of the Madrileño eating experience – bounces off the tiled walls
(pictured p152) adorned with bullfighting memorabilia. The specialty
is as much *cocido* (chickpea and
meat stew) as you can eat (€18).
Strangely, it closes when El Rastro
flea market comes to the barrio.

NAÏA RESTAURANTE
Spanish & Nouvelle Cuisine €€

☎ 91 366 27 83; www.naiarestaurante
.com, in Spanish; Plaza de la Paja 3;
⏱ 1.30-4.30pm & 8.30-11.30pm Tue-Fri,
1.30-6pm & 8.30pm-midnight Sat & Sun,
8.30pm-11.30pm Mon; Ⓜ La Latina

On the lovely Plaza de la Paja,
Naïa has a real buzz about it with
a cooking laboratory overseen
by Carlos López Reyes, delightful
modern Spanish cooking and a
chill-out lounge downstairs.

🍴 TABERNA DE ANTONIO SÁNCHEZ *Tapas* €€

☎ 91 539 78 26; Calle de Mesón des Paredes 13; ⏱ noon-4pm & 8pm-midnight Mon-Sat, noon-4pm Sun; Ⓜ Tirso de Molina; ♿

Behind one of the best-preserved old *taberna* façades in Madrid hides this gem of a traditional tapas bar famous for its Madrid specialities – *tortilla de san isidro*, *callos* (tripe), *morcilla* (blood sausage), *huevos estrellados* (fried eggs) and a host of other excellent local favourites.

🍴 TABERNA MATRITUM *Tapas* €€

☎ 91 365 82 37; www.matritum.es, in Spanish; Calle de la Cava Alta 17; ⏱ 1-4.30pm & 8.30pm-12.30am Thu-Sun, 8.30pm-12.30am Mon-Wed; Ⓜ La Latina

This little gem is reason enough to detour from the more popular Calle de la Cava Baja next door. Terrific *pinchos* (tapas), canapés and carefully chosen mains and salads (such as warm octopus and potato salad with miso dressing) are complemented by a good wine list and a cosy ambience.

🍴 TXAKOLINA *Basque & Tapas* €€

☎ 91 366 48 77; Calle de la Cava Baja 26; ⏱ 7.30pm-12.30am Mon-Thu, 7.30pm-2am Fri, noon-2am Sat & Sun; Ⓜ La Latina

It calls its abundant Basque *pintxos* (tapas) 'high cuisine in miniature' – the first part is true, but these are some of the biggest *pintxos* you'll find and some are a meal in themselves. It does wonderful things with seafood and potatoes too.

🍴 TXIRIMIRI *Tapas* €€

☎ 91 364 11 96; www.txirimiri.es, in Spanish; Calle del Humilladero 6; ⏱ 8pm-midnight Mon & Tue, noon-midnight Wed-Sun; Ⓜ La Latina

This *pintxo* bar is a great little discovery just down from the main

A SPECIAL BOUQUET

Like any old Madrid *taberna* worth its salt, Taberna de Antonio Sánchez has its share of special legends. Our favourite dates back to the early 18th century when Madrid briefly rose up against the French occupiers. Inhabitants of the barrio reportedly killed a French soldier and, to avoid reprisals, hid his body in a barrel in the bar's cellar. That would have been the end of the story, but for the fact that not only did the bar's owners keep selling wine from the barrel, but it became their most popular drop with what the owners described as 'an extraordinary bouquet'. Thankfully, you won't find it on the menu any more, but asking the bartender for '*un vino de la cuba de francés*' (a wine from the barrel of the Frenchman) still elicits a wry, knowing smile.

La Latina tapas circuit. Wonderful wines, gorgeous *pinchos* (the *tortilla de patatas* is superb) and fine risottos add up to a pretty special combination.

DRINK

La Latina has loads of bars but you know when you've entered one that really stands out. The vibe is usually intimate and brimful of people and personality. Calle de la Cava Baja, Calle de Almendro and Plaza de la Paja are the hubs of the barrio's nights out. Lavapiés is more eclectic, but there's still plenty to choose from.

CAFÉ DEL NUNCIO *Bar*
☎ 91 366 09 06; Calle de Segovia 9;
🕑 noon-1.30am Sun-Thu, noon-2.30am
Fri & Sat; Ⓜ La Latina
Café del Nuncio straggles down a stairway passage to Calle de Segovia. Despite the hum of the crowds that gather outside for one of the most agreeable *terrazas* (outdoor tables) in La Latina, this fine old bar with its 19th-century décor proves that not all Madrid nightlife is about living life at full volume.

DELIC *Café-Bar*
☎ 91 364 54 50; www.deliccafe.com,
in Spanish; Costanilla de San Andrés 14;
🕑 11am-2am Tue-Thu, 11am-2.30am
Fri-Sun & 7pm-2.30am Mon; Ⓜ La Latina
We could go on for hours about this café-bar, but we'll reduce it to

---

LA HORA DEL VERMUT

Sunday. One o'clock in the afternoon. A dark bar off Calle de la Cava Baja. In any civilised city the bar would be shut tight, but in Madrid the place is packed because it's *la hora del vermut* (vermouth hour), when friends and families head out for a quick apéritif before Sunday lunch. Sometimes referred to as *ir del Rastro* (going from El Rastro) because so many of the traditional vermouth bars are in and around the Rastro market, this Sunday tradition is deeply engrained in Madrileño culture. Some of the best bars for vermouth are along Calle de la Cava Baja (between El Rastro and Plaza Mayor), while Casa Alberto (p75) is another legendary part of this fine tradition.

---

its most basic elements: nursing an exceptionally good *mojito* (Cuban cocktail) or three on a warm summer's evening at Delic's outdoor tables on one of Madrid's prettiest plazas is one of life's great pleasures and an essential Madrid experience. Bliss.

EL EUCALIPTO *Cuban Bar*
Calle de Argumosa 4; 🕑 5pm-2am Mon-
Thu, 5pm-3am Fri & Sat, noon-midnight
Sun; Ⓜ Lavapiés; ♿
You'd be mad not to at least pass by this fine little bar with its love of all things Cuban, from the music to the clientele and the Caribbean cocktails. Not surprisingly, the *mojitos* are a cut above the average.

☿ EL VIAJERO *Bar*
☎ 91 366 90 64; Plaza de la Cebada 11; ⌚ 1pm-12.30am Tue-Thu & Sun, 1pm-1am Fri & Sat; Ⓜ La Latina

This upstairs bar requires the patience of a saint – it's busy and near-on impossible to get a table unless you're prepared to wait. But wait you should, because El Viajero is always buzzing (has been for years) and the rooftop terrace on a summer's night is pure bliss.

☿ GAUDEAMUS CAFÉ *Café-Bar*
☎ 91 528 25 94; www.gaudeamuscafe .com, in Spanish; 4th fl, Calle de Tribulete 14; ⌚ 3.30pm-midnight Mon-Fri, 8pm-midnight Sat; Ⓜ Lavapiés

Decoration that's light and airy with pop-art posters of Audrey Hepburn and James Bond. A large terrace with views over the Lavapiés rooftops. A stunning backdrop of a ruined church atop which the café sits. Gaudeamus Café is definitely a candidate for Madrid's best rooftop café-bar.

☿ LA INQUILINA *Bar*
☎ 627 511 804; Calle del Ave María 39; ⌚ 7pm-1.30am Tue-Thu, 7pm-2.30am Fri & Sat, 1pm-1am Sun; Ⓜ Lavapiés

A barrio bar in the best Lavapiés tradition, La Inquilina has friendly, all-female service, contemporary artworks by budding local artists and a cheerful, sophisticated vibe.

☿ LA TABERNA CHICA *Bar*
☎ 91 364 53 48; Costanilla de San Pedro 7; ⌚ 8pm-1.30am Mon-Thu, 1.30pm-2am Fri-Sun; Ⓜ La Latina

Most of those who come to this narrow little bar are after one

Everything tastes better amid beautiful décor and many Madrid restaurants deliver that in spades!

thing – the famous Santa Teresa rum that comes served in an extra-large mug. The music is chill-out with a nod to lounge, which makes it an ideal pit stop if you're hoping for conversation.

▼ TABERNA TEMPRANILLO
Bar

☎ 91 364 15 32; Calle de la Cava Baja 38; ⏰ 8pm-midnight Mon, 1-3.30pm & 8pm-midnight Tue-Sun ; Ⓜ La Latina
You could come here for the tapas, but we recommend Taberna Tempranillo primarily for its wines – its selection puts most Spanish bars to shame. It's not a late-night place, but it's always packed with an early evening crowd and on Sundays after El Rastro. Its fluted columns and floor-to-ceiling wine rack add a certain old-world charm.

⭐ PLAY

If you like your nights out to be shared more with Madrileños than tourists, there are a couple of options north of Plaza de la Lavapiés.

⬛ CASA PATAS *Flamenco*
☎ 91 369 04 96; www.casapatas.com, in Spanish; Calle de Cañizares 10; admission €32; ⏰ shows 10.30pm Mon-Thu, 9pm & midnight Fri & Sat; Ⓜ Antón Martín
One of the top flamenco stages in Madrid, this *tablao* (restaurant

with a flemenco floorshow) is a good place for an introduction to the art. Although it's geared toward tourists, locals stop by for a soul-filling session of passionate music and dance. Booking ahead is a must.

⬛ EL JUGLAR *Nightclub*
☎ 91 528 43 81; www.salajuglar.com, in Spanish; Calle de Lavapiés 37; admission free-€10; ⏰ 9pm-3am Sun-Wed, 9pm-3.30am Thu-Sat; Ⓜ Lavapiés
One of the most creative clubs in Madrid, El Juglar draws an unpretentious crowd looking for down-tempo jazz and soul beats, with fiery nods to flamenco at 10pm on Sunday and the first Wednesday of every month. There are more frenetic clubs, but none as agreeable.

⬛ LA ESCALERA DE JACOB
Live Music

☎ 649 423 254; www.laescaleradejacob .es, in Spanish; Calle de Lavapiés 11; admission €7-10; ⏰ 8pm-3am Wed-Sat; Ⓜ Antón Martín or Tirso de Molina
'Jacob's Ladder' offers up an eclectic mix of live music, theatre, comedy and cabaret, as well as being a great bar. This offbeat approach draws an equally eclectic cross-section of young Madrileños.

>HUERTAS & ATOCHA

Madrid at full volume. Madrid at full speed. Welcome to Huertas, one of the most buzzing, culturally rich and noisiest barrios in Madrid. At the centre of it all lies Plaza de Santa Ana, which is as sophisticated by day with its outdoor tables as it is raucous and infectiously alive by night. Between Plaza de Santa Ana and Plaza de la Puerta del Sol are dozens of excellent tapas bars. Down the hill to the east, especially along Calle de Echegaray and Calle de las Huertas, is a smorgasbord of restaurants, live flamenco and jazz venues, and bars. This latter area is also home to the Barrio de las Letras (Barrio of Letters) where many a great Spanish writer once lived, while down the hill towards the landmark Antigua Estación de Atocha is the Centro de Arte Reina Sofía, one of Madrid's 'Big Three' art galleries.

HUERTAS & ATOCHA

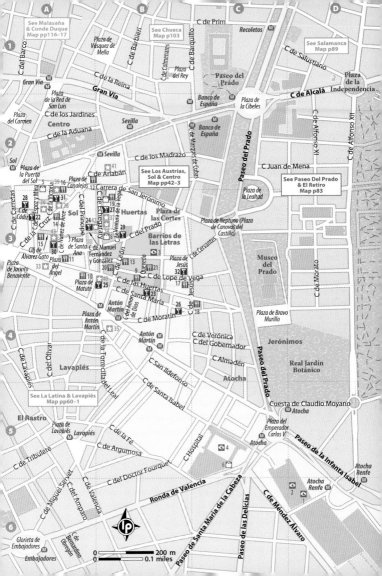

A

- See Malasaña & Conde Duque Map pp116–17
- Plaza de Vásquez de Mella
- Plaza del Barco
- Gran Vía
- Plaza de la Red de San Luis
- Plaza del Carmen
- Centro
- C de la Aduana
- Sol
- Plaza de la Puerta del Sol
- Plaza de Canalejas
- C de Cádiz
- Sol
- Plaza de Santa Ana
- C de Manuel Fernández y González
- C de Álvarez Gato
- Plaza del Ángel
- Plaza de Jacinto Benavente
- Plaza de Matute
- Antón Martín
- Plaza de Antón Martín
- Lavapiés
- El Rastro
- Plaza de Lavapiés
- Lavapiés
- C de Tribulete
- C de Miguel Servet
- C de Bernardino Obregón
- Glorieta de Embajadores
- Embajadores

B

- See Chueca Map p103
- C de Barbieri
- C de Colmenares
- Plaza del Rey
- C de la Reina
- Gran Vía
- C de los Jardines
- Sevilla
- Sevilla
- C de los Madrazo
- C de Arlabán
- Carrera de San Jerónimo
- Huertas
- Plaza de las Cortes
- Barrios de las Letras
- C del Prado
- C de las Huertas
- C de Santa María
- C de Moratín
- Antón Martín
- C San Ildefonso
- C de Santa Isabel
- C de la Fé
- C de Argumosa
- C del Doctor Fourquet
- Ronda de Valencia

C

- C de Prim
- Recoletos
- Paseo del Prado
- Banco de España
- Plaza de la Cibeles
- Banco de España
- Plaza de las Cortes
- Plaza de Neptuno (Plaza de Cánovas del Castillo)
- Plaza de la Lealtad
- Plaza de Jesús
- C de Lope de Vega
- C de Verónica
- C del Gobernador
- C Almadén
- Atocha
- C Hospital
- Plaza del Emperador Carlos V
- Atocha
- Paseo de las Delicias
- Paseo de Santa María de la Cabeza
- C de Méndez Álvaro

D

- See Salamanca Map p89
- C de Salustiano
- Plaza de la Independencia
- C de Alcalá
- C de Alfonso XII
- C de Alfonso XI
- C Juan de Mena
- See Paseo Del Prado & El Retiro Map p83
- Museo del Prado
- C de Morato
- Jerónimos
- Real Jardín Botánico
- Cuesta de Claudio Moyano
- Atocha
- Paseo del Prado
- Plaza de Bravo Murillo
- Paseo de la Infanta Isabel
- Atocha Renfe
- Atocha Renfe

See Los Austrias, Sol & Centro Map pp42–3

0   200 m
0   0.1 miles

BARRIOS

HUERTAS & ATOCHA

👁 SEE

🖸 11 MARCH 2004 MEMORIAL

1st fl, Estación de Atocha; admission free; 🕐 **10am-2pm & 4-8pm;** Ⓜ **Atocha Renfe**
This moving monument to the victims of the worst terrorist attack on European soil at Atocha station is partially visible from the street, but the glass tower is best viewed from below. A glass panel shows the names of those killed while the airy glass-and-perspex tower is inscribed with the messages of condolence left by well-wishers in a number of languages in the immediate aftermath of the attack. It's simple but powerful. You may have to queue to enter.

RETURNING HOME?

Painted by Picasso in France, *Guernica* migrated from France to New York's Museum of Modern Art. In 1981 it finally made its way to Spain in keeping with Picasso's wish that *Guernica* return to Spanish shores and be displayed in the Museo del Prado once democracy had been restored. It moved across Paseo del Prado to the Reina Sofía in 1992, but there have been repeated calls for the painting to be moved to the Basque Country (most recently in 2006 for a temporary exhibition). The curators of the Centro de Arte Reina Sofía argue that the painting is too fragile to be moved.

🖸 ANTIGUA ESTACIÓN DE ATOCHA

Plaza del Emperador Carlos V; Ⓜ **Atocha Renfe**
This iron-and-glass relic from the 19th century resonates with the grand old European train stations of another age.

🖸 CASA DE LOPE DE VEGA

☎ **91 429 92 16; Calle de Cervantes 11; admission free;** 🕐 **guided visits every 30 mins 10am-2pm;** Ⓜ **Antón Martín**
The former home of one of history's greatest (and most colourful) Spanish-language playwrights is filled with memorabilia related to his life and times, and there's a tranquil garden out the back.

🖸 CENTRO DE ARTE REINA SOFÍA

☎ **91 774 10 00; www.museoreinasofia .es; Calle de Santa Isabel 52; adult/ student/child under 18 yr & senior over 65 yr €6/4/free;** 🕐 **10am-9pm Mon & Wed-Sat, 10am-2.30pm Sun;** Ⓜ **Atocha**
The state-of-the-art Reina Sofía is a shining example of that Spanish flair for converting old-world architecture to meet the needs of a dynamic modern-art collection. The gallery's recent glass-and-steel extension along the western tip of the Plaza del Emperador Carlos V is one of Madrid's modern architectural highlights, while the collection of 20th-century, mostly

Be illuminated by Spanish art at Centro de Arte Reina Sofía

Spanish art is outstanding. The Reina Sofía's main claim to fame is as the home of Picasso's *Guernica*, but there's so much more to catch the eye here. See p16 for details.

🛍 SHOP

Although there are some intriguing little boutiques tucked away in the Barrio del las Letras, you wouldn't really come to Huertas or Atocha for the shopping. Most of what's of interest is closer to the Plaza de la Puerta del Sol.

🛍 GIL *Souvenirs*
☎ 91 521 25 49; Carrera de San Jerónimo 2; ⏰ 9.30am-1.30pm & 4.30-8pm Mon-Sat; Ⓜ Sol

Exquisitely fringed and embroidered *mantones* and *mantoncillos* (traditional Spanish shawls worn by women on grand occasions) and delicate *mantillas* (Spanish veils) are the speciality of this enduring Madrid monument to old Spanish style. The service hasn't changed in years and that's no bad thing.

🛍 LIBRERÍA DE CENTRO DE ARTE REINA SOFÍA
Art Bookshop
☎ 91 787 87 82; www.lacentral.com; Ronda de Atocha 2; ⏰ 10am-9pm Mon & Wed-Sat, 10am-2.30pm Sun; Ⓜ Atocha
Part of the stunning extension to the Centro de Arte Reina Sofía, this outstanding shop is Madrid's

best gallery bookshop, with a range of posters and postcards as well.

🗋 LOMOGRAPHY *Photography*
☎ 91 369 17 99; www.lomospain .com, in Spanish; Calle de Echegaray 5; 🕙 11am-8.30pm Mon-Fri & 11am-2pm Sat; Ⓜ Sevilla or Sol

Dedicated to a Russian Kompakt camera that has acquired cult status for zany colours, fish-eye lenses and anticool clunkiness, this eclectic shop sells the cameras (an original will set you back €295) as well as offbeat design items.

🗋 MARÍA CABELLO
Wines
☎ 91 429 60 88; Calle de Echegaray 19; 🕙 9.30am-2.30pm & 5.30-9pm Mon-Fri, 10am-2.30pm & 6.30-9.30pm Sat; Ⓜ Sol or Antón Martín

You'll never be able to buy your wine at the supermarket again after visiting this jewel of an old wine store. The 1913 fresco on the ceiling may have faded but the family that runs this store have all the time in the world, not to mention a razor-sharp memory for wines. They know just what you're looking for.

There's a bottle with your name on it at María Cabello wine shop

🍴 EAT

Huertas is one of those self-contained barrios where you could spend an entire day and night without feeling the need to leave, and central to this idea are its outstanding restaurants. The choice ranges from Basque or Galician to international. A cosy ambience is this barrio's speciality.

🍴 A TASCA DO BACALHAU PORTUGUÊS
Portuguese   €€€

☎ 91 429 56 75; Calle de Lope de Vega 14; ⏱ 1.30-4.30pm & 8.30pm-12.30am Tue-Sat, 1.30-4.30pm Sun; Ⓜ Antón Martín; ♿ 🚼

One of very few authentically Portuguese restaurants in Madrid, A Tasca do Bacalhau doesn't have a particularly extensive menu, but it's dominated by excellent *bacalhau* (cod) and rice dishes. It's pricey but if you're not familiar with Portuguese cooking, this is a good place to have your first taste.

🍴 CASA ALBERTO
Spanish & Tapas   €€

☎ 91 429 93 56; www.casaalberto.es; Calle de las Huertas 18; ⏱ noon-1.30am Tue-Sat, noon-4pm Sun; Ⓜ Antón Martín

One of the most atmospheric old *tabernas* (taverns) of Madrid, Casa Alberto has been around since 1827. The secret to its staying power is vermouth *(vermut)* on tap, excellent tapas with no frilly innovations that have come to characterise Spanish tapas (*jamón* – ham, Manchego cheese and anchovies are recurring themes here), and fine sit-down meals.

🍴 EL LATERAL *Tapas*   €€

☎ 91 420 15 82; www.cadenalateral .es, in Spanish; Plaza de Santa Ana 12; ⏱ noon-1am; Ⓜ Tribunal

Our pick of the tapas bars surrounding Plaza de Santa Ana, El Lateral does terrific *pinchos* (tapas), the perfect accompaniment to the fine wines on offer. At around €3.50 per *pincho,* you could easily pass an evening here savouring every bite. Service is restaurant-standard, rather than your average tapas-bar brusqueness.

🍴 LA FINCA DE SUSANA
Mediterranean   €€

☎ 91 369 35 57; Calle de Arlabán 4; ⏱ 1-3.45pm & 8.30-11.45pm; Ⓜ Sevilla

The classy ambience, bargain prices, innovative approach to traditional food and tastefully chic décor have made this one of Madrid's most enduringly popular restaurants. The word on the street is that it's not quite what it was, but we're not sure we agree. It doesn't take reservations and there's still often a queue outside.

🍴 LA PIOLA *Italian & Café* €

Calle de León 9; 🕐 **10am-1am Mon-Thu, 10am-2.30am Fri, 11am-2.30am Sat;** Ⓜ **Antón Martín;** 🚻 🚹

This charming Italian place serves everything from breakfast to spirits. In between, the small range of pasta on offer is well priced and filled with subtle flavours. In addition to the simple tables and bar stools, there's a sofa that has to be the best seat in the house.

🍴 LA TRUCHA *Tapas* €€

☎ **91 532 08 82; Calle de Núñez de Arce 6;** 🕐 **12.30-4pm & 7.30pm-midnight Tue-Sat;** Ⓜ **Sol**

'The Trout' is one of Madrid's great tapas bars and the faux-Andalucian décor leaves little doubt as to where its allegiances lie. The counter is loaded with enticing tapas choices and the bar staff will have their own idea about what's good to try – listen to them because they know their tapas.

🍴 LAS BRAVAS *Tapas* €€

☎ **91 532 26 20; Cnr Calle de Espoz y Mina & Callejón de Álvarez Gato;** 🕐 **12.30-3.45pm & 7.30pm-midnight;** Ⓜ **Sol**

Famed for having some of the best *patatas bravas* (fried potatoes with spicy tomato sauce) and *tortilla de patata* (Spanish tortilla) in town, Las Bravas is one of those Spanish bars where the waiters shout and the crowd crescendoes to an agreeable roar.

🍴 LHARDY *Spanish* €€€

☎ **91 522 22 07; www.lhardy.com; Carrera de San Jerónimo 8;** 🕐 **1-3.30pm & 8.30-11pm Mon-Sat, 1-3.30pm Sun, closed Aug;** Ⓜ **Sevilla**

Takeaway gourmet tapas to make your dinner-party guests swoon downstairs, and high-quality Madrid specialities in the dining room upstairs, Lhardy has found the secret to staying popular in Madrid. Service is as impeccable as the food.

🍴 LOS GATOS *Tapas* €€

☎ **91 429 30 67; Calle de Jesús 2;** 🕐 **noon-1am Sun-Thu, noon-2am Fri & Sat;** Ⓜ **Antón Martín**

Tapas you can point to without deciphering the menu and eclectic old-world décor (bullfighting memorabilia, an old petrol pump and a skeleton fresco) make this a popular choice down Huertas hill. Its most popular order are the *tostas* (tapas on toast) which, we have to say, are rather delicious. It's a good option if you're gallery-hopping along Paseo del Prado.

🍴 MACEIRAS *Galician* €€

☎ **91 429 15 84; Calle de las Huertas 66;** 🕐 **8.30pm-12.45am Tue, 1.15-4.15pm & 8.30pm-12.45am Wed, Thu, Sun & Mon, until 1.15am Fri & Sat;** Ⓜ **Antón Martín**

Galician tapas (think octopus, green peppers etc) never tasted so good as in this agreeably rustic bar down towards the bottom of the

Huertas hill. The simple wooden tables, loyal customers and handy location make this a fine place to rest after (or en route to) the museums along the Paseo del Prado.

🍴 RESTAURANTE INTEGRAL ARTEMISA *Vegetarian* €€
☎ 91 429 50 92; Calle de Ventura de la Vega 4; ⏰ 1.30-4pm & 9pm-midnight; Ⓜ Sevilla; ♿ Ⓥ

With a couple of options for meat-eaters, this mostly vegetarian restaurant does a brisk trade with its salads, moussaka and rice dishes. The décor is simple and the service no-nonsense.

🍴 VINOS GONZÁLEZ
Deli & Café €€
☎ 91 429 56 18; pcarmona@eresmas .net; Calle de León 12; ⏰ 9am-midnight Tue-Thu, 9am-1am Fri & Sat, varies in Jul & Aug; Ⓜ Antón Martín; ♿ ⛄

Ever dreamed of a deli where you could choose a tasty morsel and sit down and eat it right there? Well, here you can. On offer is a huge, tempting array of cheeses, cured meats and other typically Spanish delicacies. It has informal, café-style tables and also does takeaway.

🍴 ZERAÍN *Basque* €€
☎ 91 429 79 09; www.restaurante -vasco-zerain-sidreria.es, in Spanish; Calle de Quevedo 3; ⏰ 1.30-4pm & 8.30pm-midnight Mon-Sat, 1.30-4pm Sun; Ⓜ Antón Martín

In the heart of the Barrio de las Letras, this sophisticated Basque cider house gets rave reviews for its steaks, *bacalao* (dried salted codfish) and other Basque staples, while the service is faultless. It's not cheap, but it's classy and worth every euro.

🍸 DRINK

You may eat well in Huertas, but drinking is really what the barrio and its visitors excel at. Bars are everywhere, from Sol to the lower end of Huertas. Your standard Huertas bar has touts outside offering a cheap first drink and we haven't bothered to list these as they're a dime a dozen. In any event, they'll find you before you find them.

🍸 CAFÉ DEL SOUL *Bar*
☎ 91 523 16 06; Calle de Espoz y Mina 14; ⏰ 4pm-2am Mon-Fri, noon-3am Sat, noon-2am Sun; Ⓜ Sol

Cocktails for €6 are a big selling point these days in Madrid. If you add chill-out music and curious décor with bench-style seating and softly lit Moroccan lamps, Café del Soul is a decent choice for a quiet night out.

🍸 DOS GARDENIAS *Lounge Bar*
Calle de Santa María 13; ⏰ 8pm-2.30am Mon-Sat, 5pm-2.30am Sun; Ⓜ Antón Martín; ♿

When Huertas starts to overwhelm, this soothing little bar is the perfect antidote. The flamenco and other chill-out music ensures a down-tempo mood, while sofas, softly lit colours and some of the best *mojitos* (Cuban cocktail) in the barrio make this the perfect place to ease yourself into or out of the night.

▼ EL CALLEJÓN *Flamenco Bar*
Calle de Manuel Fernández y González 5; ☽ **7.30pm-2.30am Sun-Thu, 7.30pm-3.30am Fri & Sat;** Ⓜ **Sevilla or Antón Martín;** ♿
Tucked in between Viva Madrid and the Plaza de Santa Ana, the tiny El Callejón lives and breathes flamenco from the music coming from the sound system to the stars of *cante jondo* (deep flamenco song) who adorn the walls. The clientele is overwhelmingly local and even includes flamenco stars who recognise authentic flamenco when they hear it.

▼ EL IMPERFECTO *Bar*
☎ **91 366 72 11; Plaza de Matute 2;** ☽ **3pm-2am Mon-Thu, 3pm-2.30am Fri & Sat;** Ⓜ **Antón Martín**
Its name notwithstanding, the 'Imperfect One' is our ideal Huertas bar, with live jazz on some Tuesdays (and sometimes other nights) and a drinks menu as long as a saxophone, ranging from cocktails and spirits to milkshakes, teas and creative coffees. It draws a young professional crowd with great background music.

▼ JAZZ BAR *Jazz Bar*
☎ **91 429 70 31; Calle de Moratín 35;** ☽ **3pm-2.30am Sun-Thu, 3pm-3.30am Fri & Sat;** Ⓜ **Antón Martín;** ♿ ⚦
Jazz aficionados will love this place for its endless jazz soundtrack and private booths (at last, a bar that has gone for privacy rather than trying to cram too many people in) and there's plenty of greenery to keep you cheerful.

▼ LA VENENCIA *Bar*
☎ **91 429 73 13; Calle de Echegaray 7;** ☽ **1-3.30pm & 7.30pm-1.30am Sun-Thu, 1-3.30pm & 7.30pm-2.30am Fri & Sat;** Ⓜ **Sol**
If you like your sherry straight from the wooden barrel, La Venencia will quickly become your favourite Madrid bar. There's no music, no flashy decorations – it's all about you, your *fino* (sherry) and your friends.

▼ MALASPINA *Bar*
☎ **91 523 40 24; Calle de Cádiz 9;** ☽ **11am-2am Sun-Thu, 11am-2.30am Fri & Sat;** Ⓜ **Sol**
Although it serves inviting tapas throughout the day, we like this cosy place with its wooden tables and semirustic décor as a mellow place for a quiet one as you head home for an early night. Many of the bars in this area lack character or have sold their soul to the god of tourism. This place is different.

Y ØLSEN *Bar & Restaurant*

☎ 91 429 36 59; www.olsenmadrid.com;
Calle del Prado 15; ⏱ 1-5pm & 8pm-2am,
till 2.30am Fri & Sat; Ⓜ Anton Martín
This classy, clean-lined bar-
restaurant is a temple to Nordic
minimalism and to vodka, with
a menu devoted solely to the
latter that features more than 80
varieties, not to mention plenty of
vodka-dominated cocktails. You'll
hate vodka the next day, but Madrid is all about living for the night.

Y PENTHOUSE
Cocktail Bar

☎ 91 701 60 20; 7th fl, Plaza de Santa
Ana 14; ⏱ 9pm-2am Sun-Wed, 9pm-3am
Thu-Sat; Ⓜ Antón Martín or Sol
High above Plaza de Santa Ana, this
sybaritic rooftop cocktail bar has
terrific views over Madrid's rooftops.
It's a sophisticated place with chill-
out areas strewn with cushions, but
prices are suitably high.

Y TABERNA ALHAMBRA *Bar*

☎ 91 521 07 08; www.tabernaalham
bra.es, in Spanish; Calle de Victoria 9;
⏱ 11am-1.30am Sun-Wed, 11am-2am
Thu, 11am-3.30am Fri & Sat; Ⓜ Sol
There can be a certain sameness
about the bars between Sol and
Huertas, which is why this fine old
taberna stands out. The striking
façade, Mudéjar decoration and
beautiful tilework of the interior
complements a vibe that's cool,

casual and busy. Late at night, there
are some fine flamenco tunes.

Y TABERNA DE DOLORES *Bar*

☎ 91 429 22 43; Plaza de Jesús 4;
⏱ 11am-1am Sun-Thu, 11am-2am Fri &
Sat; Ⓜ Antón Martín
Old bottles and beer mugs line
the shelves behind the bar at this
Madrid institution, known for its
blue-and-white tiled exterior and
for an older, 30-something crowd.
You can get good house wine and
some of Madrid's best beer for
€1.75 a pop.

Y VIVA MADRID *Bar*

☎ 91 429 36 40; www.barvivamadrid
.com; Calle de Manuel Fernández y
González 7; ⏱ 1pm-2.30am Sun-Thu,
1pm-3am Fri & Sat; Ⓜ Antón Martín or Sol
The tiled façade of Viva Madrid is
one of Madrid's most recognisable,
and is an essential landmark on the
Huertas nightlife scene. It's packed
to the rafters on weekends and you
come here as much for some of
the best *mojitos* in town as for the
casual, always friendly atmosphere.

⭐ PLAY

Huertas stays open late and at
first look can seem swamped with
hedonism catering to the latest
music and an often-younger
crowd. Look a little harder and
you'll find sophisticated live-music
venues and nightclubs for the
more discerning among you.

⭐ CINEMAS & THEATRES

⭐ CINE DORÉ *Cinema*
☎ 91 369 11 25; Calle de Santa Isabel 3; Ⓜ Antón Martín

This wonderful old cinema is home to the Filmoteca Nacional (National Film Library) and shows classics for just €1.50. Four movies are shown nightly; the first one at 5.30pm, the last around 10pm.

⭐ LIVE MUSIC

⭐ CAFÉ CENTRAL *Live Jazz*
☎ 91 369 41 43; www.cafecentralmadrid .com; Plaza del Ángel 10; admission €8-12; ⏱ 1.30pm-2.30am Sun-Thu, 1.30pm-3.30am Fri & Sat; Ⓜ Antón Martín or Sol

This bar is a study in Art Deco elegance and it morphs into one of Madrid's best jazz venues after 10pm. Performances are of the highest quality and include everything from Latin jazz to fusion, tango and classic jazz.

⭐ CARDAMOMO *Flamenco*
☎ 91 369 07 57; www.cardamomo.net; Calle de Echegaray 15; admission €25; ⏱ 9pm-3.30am; Ⓜ Sevilla

One of the spiritual homes of flamenco in Madrid, Cardamomo is a dark, smoky bar that draws a knowledgeable crowd. It has lost a little atmosphere after a recent change of owner, but the flamenco is top-notch and there are nightly shows at 10pm.

⭐ LA BOCA DEL LOBO
Live Music
☎ 91 429 70 13; www.labocadelobo .com; Calle de Echegaray 11; admission €5-7; ⏱ 9.30pm-3am; Ⓜ Sol

If you like your live music in a setting that's sometimes intimate and sometimes rowdy, head for the 'Wolf's Mouth', which is known for offering mostly rock and alternative concerts, with occasional country and jazz thrown in. Concerts are held at least three times a week, usually on Wednesday, Thursday and/or Friday.

⭐ LA FONTANA DE ORO
Live Music
☎ 91 531 04 20; Calle de Victoria 1; admission free; ⏱ 1pm-6am; Ⓜ Sol

This Irish bar lays claim to being the oldest bar in Madrid, dating back to 1789. Mentioned in *La Fontana de Oro,* the novel by Benito Pérez Galdós, the upstairs bar is dedicated in part to the author and it's here that nightly Celtic or rock groups take to the stage at 10pm.

⭐ POPULART *Live Jazz*
☎ 91 429 84 07; www.populart.es; Calle de las Huertas 22; admission free; ⏱ 6pm-2.30am Mon-Fri, 6pm-3.30am Fri & Sat; Ⓜ Antón Martín or Sol

One of Madrid's classic jazz clubs, this place offers a low-key atmosphere and top-quality music. The shows start at 11pm, but if you want a seat, get here early. There's no cover charge, and drinks cost €7 and up.

⭐ SOL Y SOMBRA *Live Music*
☎ 91 542 81 93; www.solysombra .name/; Calle de Echegaray 18; admission free-€30; ⏱ 10pm-3.30am; Ⓜ Sevilla
Sol y Sombra is the work of designer Tomás Alía and, after a number of manifestations, has settled into a semi-upmarket nightclub with swirling colours, danceable music, creative lighting and expensive drinks. The atmosphere can depend on the night, as does the strictness of the door policy, but it's always worth a look.

⭐ NIGHTCLUBS
⭐ EL SON *Latin Nightclub*
☎ 91 523 26 09; Calle de Victoria 6; admission incl first drink €8; ⏱ 9.30pm-6am; Ⓜ Sol; ♿
If you're looking for salsa, merengue or some sexy tangos, look no further than El Son. This is the top place in town for Latin music and it's very popular with Madrid's South and Central American population. Live concerts Monday through Thursday keep the place packed all week long.

⭐ LA CARTUJA *Nightclub*
☎ 91 521 55 89; Calle de la Cruz 10; ⏱ 11pm-5.30am; Ⓜ Sol or Sevilla

A real mixed bag of styles, the three bars of La Cartuja make it a late-night Huertas favourite with many. The decoration is Andalucian, while the music is a mix of Spanish and Latin American tunes with salsa on Wednesday nights.

⭐ ROOM CLUB *Nightclub*
☎ 91 531 63 78; www.theroomclub .com, in Spanish; Calle de Arlabán 7; ⏱ 12.30-6am Thu-Sat; Ⓜ Sevilla
DJ Ángel García (on Friday) is one of Madrid's best, and don't even think about arriving after 3am – there simply won't be room and those inside have no intention of leaving until dawn. The great visuals would leave you cross-eyed if you weren't already in this vibrant, heady place.

⭐ VILLA ROSA *Nightclub*
☎ 91 521 36 89; www.villarosaflamenco .es, in Spanish; Plaza de Santa Ana 15; admission free-€30; ⏱ 11.30pm-4am Wed, 11.30pm-5am Thu, 11.30pm-6am Fri & Sat; Ⓜ Sol
The extraordinary tiled façade of this long-standing nightclub is a tourist attraction in itself. On many Friday and Saturday nights at 9.30pm it opens earlier for terrific live flamenco. When there's no flamenco happening, it's a fairly standard nightclub with none-too-challenging music you can't help but dance to.

>PASEO DEL PRADO & EL RETIRO

Paseo del Prado, the southward extension of Paseo de la Castellana and Paseo de los Recoletos, is Madrid's grandest boulevard. Lined with greenery and stately former palaces, this is an area that you come to see, rather than to shop, eat or drink. The highlights along the Paseo are all about art – the Museo del Prado, one of Europe's most important art galleries, and the hugely impressive Museo Thyssen-Bornemisza, are among Madrid's must-sees. There is something suitably sedate about the streets surrounding the Paseo and the patrician air of high culture finds its expression in exclusive restaurants and a church, Iglesia de San Jerónimo El Real, that's favoured by royalty. The greenery that runs down the centre of the boulevard, overflowing from the Real Jardín Botánico and running to the horizon up the hill in the Parque del Buen Retiro, helps make this one of Madrid's most agreeable barrios.

PASEO DEL PRADO & EL RETIRO

◉ SEE
Caixa Forum 1 A5
Iglesia de San Jerónimo
El Real 2 B4
Museo del Prado 3 A4
Museo Thyssen-
Bornemisza 4 A3
Parque del Buen
Retiro 5 B4
Plaza de la Cibeles 6 A2

Puerta de Alcalá 7 B2
Real Jardín Botánico 8 A5

⌂ SHOP
Cuesta de Moyano
Bookstalls 9 B5

🍴 EAT
Club 31 ....10 B2
La Vaca Verónica 11 A4

▼ DRINK
Tabernilla
Modernilla 12 A4

★ PLAY
Kapital 13 A5

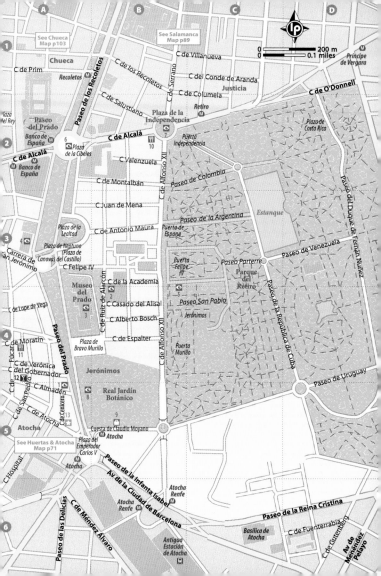

SEE

CAIXA FORUM

☎ 91 330 73 00; www.fundacio.lacaixa
.es, in Spanish; Paseo del Prado 36; admission free; ⏱ 10am-10pm; Ⓜ Serrano
Seeming to hover above the
ground, this extraordinary brick
edifice, topped by what looks like
rusted iron, sits alongside the *jardín
colgante* (hanging garden), a lush
vertical wall of greenery. Inside are
four floors of exhibition and performance space awash in stainless
steel and with soaring ceilings.

IGLESIA DE SAN JERÓNIMO EL REAL

☎ 91 420 35 78; Calle de Ruiz de Alarcón;
admission free; ⏱ 10am-1pm & 5-8pm
Mon-Sat; Ⓜ Atocha
Tucked away behind the Museo
del Prado, the favourite chapel of
Spanish royalty is awash in mock-
Isabelline splendour. King Juan
Carlos I was crowned here in 1975
upon the death of Franco.

MUSEO DEL PRADO

☎ 91 330 28 00; www.museodelprado
.es; Paseo del Prado; adult/student/ under
18 yr & EU seniors over 65 yr €8/4/free, free
to all 6-8pm Tue-Sat, 5-8pm Sun; ⏱ 9am-
8pm Tue-Sun; Ⓜ Banco de España
One of the finest art galleries in
the world, the Museo del Prado
warrants as much time and as
many visits as you can spare.

Home to masterpieces by Goya,
Velázquez and a host of European
masters, it's a stand-out highlight
of Madrid. See p12 for more
information.

MUSEO THYSSEN-BORNEMISZA

☎ 91 369 01 51; www.museothyssen.org;
Paseo del Prado 8; adult/student & senior/
child €8/5.50/free, temporary exhibitions
adult/student & senior/child under 12 yr
€5/3/free, headset guide €3; ⏱ 10am-
7pm Tue-Sun; Ⓜ Banco de España
In the rush to the Prado or Reina
Sofía, many visitors to Madrid find
the Museo Thyssen-Bornemisza
to be a road too far. Bad mistake,
for the Thyssen ends up being

Awe strikes you at Iglesia de San Jerónimo El Real

THE THYSSEN-BORNEMISZA LEGEND

The collection held in the Museo Thyssen-Bornemisza is a very Spanish story that has a celebrity love affair at its heart. The paintings held in the museum are the legacy of Baron Thyssen-Bornemisza, a German-Hungarian magnate. Spain managed to acquire the prestigious collection when the baron married Carmen Tita Cervera, a former Miss España and ex-wife of Lex Barker (of Tarzan fame). The deal was sealed when the Spanish government offered to overhaul the neoclassical Palacio de Villahermosa specifically to house the collection. Although the baron died in 2002, his glamorous wife has shown that she has learned much from the collecting nous of her late husband. In early 2000 the museum acquired two adjoining buildings, which have been joined to house approximately half of the collection of Carmen Thyssen-Bornemisza.

When Madrid City Council announced plans in April 2006 to reroute the traffic lanes in front of the Museo del Prado on the eastern side of the Paseo del Prado so that they ran past the Thyssen, the baroness threatened to publicly chain herself to a tree if the plan went ahead. The prospect of taking on one of Madrid's favourite daughters proved too much for the council, who quietly shelved the plans.

many people's favourite Madrid gallery. Where the other two allow you to focus on bodies of work from the great painters, the Thyssen gives you a stunning overview that appeals to the lay art-lover. Where else in the world can you see most of the finest European painters in history – including Tintoretto, Titian, Caravaggio, Canaletto, Cezanne, Monet, Sisley, Matisse, Toulouse-Lautrec, Renoir, Pissarro, Degas, Constable, Van Gogh, Picasso and Dalí – under one roof?

ⓒ PARQUE DEL BUEN RETIRO
admission free; ⌚ 6am-midnight May-Sep, 6am-10pm Oct-Apr; Ⓜ Retiro or Príncipe de Vergara

The wonderful gardens of El Retiro are littered with marble monuments, landscaped lawns, the occasional elegant building and abundant greenery. Quiet and contemplative during the week, El Retiro is transformed on weekends when people flock here from all over the city. For more information, see p17.

ⓒ PLAZA DE LA CIBELES
Ⓜ **Banco de España**
Plaza de la Cibeles perfectly evokes the splendour of imperial Madrid. The astonishing early-20th-century Palacio de Comunicaciones, with Gothic and Renaissance touches, overlooks the plaza from the southeast, while Puerta de Alcalá

RIOTING FOR ART

Madrid must be the only city in the world where a near-riot was caused by an art exhibition. In 1990 the Prado brought an unprecedented number of works by Velázquez out of storage. More than half a million visitors came, but when the doors closed on the last day, several hundred people were still outside waiting in the rain. They chanted, they shouted and they banged on the doors with their umbrellas. The gallery was reopened, but queues kept forming and when the doors shut on the exhibition for good at 10.30pm, furious art-lovers clashed with police.

looks down from the northeast. The spectacular fountain of the goddess Cybele is the centrepiece. This is also where Real Madrid fans traditionally celebrate victories.

PUERTA DE ALCALÁ

Plaza de la Independéncia; M Retiro
This stunning triumphal gate was once the main entrance to the city on the road leading east to Alcaláa de Henares. It is best viewed from Plaza de la Cibeles (p85). From the east the views through the arch down towards central Madrid are similarly special.

REAL JARDÍN BOTÁNICO

☎ 91 420 30 17; www.rjb.csic.es; Plaza de Bravo Murillo 2; adult/student/senior & child under 11 yr €2/1/free; ⏱ 10am-9pm May-Aug, 10am-8pm Apr & Sep, 10am-7pm Oct & Mar, 10am-6pm Nov-Feb; M Atocha
Madrid's botanical gardens are a leafy oasis in the centre of town, with 30,000 species crammed into an 8-hectare area that feels somehow isolated from the clamour of downtown Madrid.

SHOP

CUESTA DE MOYANO BOOKSTALLS *Second-Hand Books*

Calle de Claudio Moyano; ⏱ **9am-sunset Mon-Sat, 9am-2pm Sun; M Atocha**
Madrid's answer to the booksellers that line the Seine in Paris, these second-hand bookstalls are an enduring Madrid landmark. Most titles are in Spanish but there's a handful of offerings in other languages. There are more than a dozen stalls climbing the hill and opening hours vary, with many closing between 2pm and 5pm, especially in summer.

EAT

There are very few good places to eat along Paseo del Prado – head into the streets just back from the boulevard.

CLUB 31 *Spanish*   €€€

☎ 91 531 00 92; www.club31.net, in Spanish; Calle de Alcalá 58; ⏱ 1.30-4pm & 9pm-midnight Sep-Jul; M Retiro
An old Madrid classic, Club 31 has

a vaguely contemporary design with long black seats, leaning wall mirrors and bright white designer lamps hanging from the ceiling, but the cuisine is classic. The accent is on fish and venison, with the occasional modern touch (such as the lobster soufflé). Last time we ate here, royalty was at the next table.

LA VACA VERÓNICA
Home-Cooking €€

☎ 91 429 78 27; www.lavacaveronica.es, in Spanish; Calle de Moratín 38; ⏱ 1-4.30pm & 8.30pm-12.30am Mon-Sat, 1-4.30pm Sun; Ⓜ Antón Martín; ♿

Plenty of red meat and salads are the staples at this long-standing local favourite in the Paseo del Prado hinterland. There's an agreeable buzz about this place most nights and the service is excellent.

🍸 DRINK
🍸 TABERNILLA MODERNILLA
Café-Bar

Calle de San Pedro 22; ⏱ 12.30-4.30pm & 7.30pm-2am Wed-Sun; Ⓜ Antón Martín

On a quiet street just back from the Paseo del Prado is this colourful but cosy split-level little bar with an artsy vibe where *mojitos*, daiquiris and piña coladas cost a reasonable €6. From time to time it also has small shows or exhibitions and it's always worth stopping by to see what's happening.

⭐ PLAY
☆ KAPITAL *Nightclub*

☎ 91 420 29 06; www.grupo-kapital .com, in Spanish; Calle de Atocha 125; admission before 1am free; ⏱ 6-10pm & midnight-6am Thu-Sun; Ⓜ Atocha

This massive, multistorey nightclub is one of Madrid's biggies with something for everyone from cocktail bars and dance music to karaoke, salsa and hip-hop. The usually international crowd is always up for a good time and House music is the dominant force, but the 3rd and 4th floors have more chilled R&B and soul, while on the 5th floor you can dance your heart out to the latest tunes.

If you've got it, shake it at Kapital

>SALAMANCA

Salamanca is Madrid's most exclusive barrio (neighbourhood), a place that resonates with old money and, increasingly, high fashion. This is the undoubted centre of Spain's thriving fashion industry, especially along Calle de Serrano and the adjacent streets, while Calle de José Ortega y Gasset is where you'll find all the top international brand-names. Not surprisingly, Salamanca is also home to some exclusive nightclubs, stylish restaurants and oh-so-upmarket bars. Put on your finest clothes and be seen.

Bordered by Paseo de los Recoletos and Paseo de la Castellana to the west and Calle de Alcalá to the south, Salamanca has the air of an exclusive enclave of sophistication, a fact reflected in its origins. Salamanca had a powerful patron in the Marqués de Salamanca, a 19th-century aristocrat and general who built Madrid's first houses with water closets, the latest domestic plumbing and water heating for bathrooms and kitchens. He also inaugurated horse-drawn tramways. In the year of his death, 1883, the streets were the first to receive electric lighting.

SALAMANCA

◎ SEE
Biblioteca Nacional 1 A4
Museo Arqueológico
Nacional 2 A4
Museo de la Escultura
Abstracta 3 B2
Museo Lázaro
Galdiano 4 B1

🛍 SHOP
Agatha Ruiz de la
Prada 5 B3
Amaya Arzuaga 6 B4
Armand Basi 7 B3
Bombonería Santa 8 B3
Camper 9 B4
Davidelfín 10 B4

De Viaje 11 B3
Ekseption & Eks 12 B4
Gallery 13 C4
Loewe 14 B4
Manolo Blahnik 15 B3
Mantequería Bravo 16 B3
Purificación García 17 B2
Uno de 50 ....(see 7)
Vinçon 18 C4

🍽 EAT
Al-Mounia 19 A5
Biotza 20 B4
El Rocío 21 C3
La Casa del Abuelo 22 C4
La Colonial de Goya ...23 B4
La Galette 24 B5
Le Café 25 A5

Mumbai Massala 26 A5
Ramses Life & Food 27 A5
Restaurante Estay 28 C4
Sula 29 B4
Wagaboo 30 B3
Zalacaín 31 A1

▾ DRINK
Centro Cubano de
España 32 B4
El Lateral 33 B3
Geographic Club 34 C4

⋆ PLAY
Almonte 35 C2
Chi Spa 36 B5
Garamond 37 B5

⊙ SEE

⊙ BIBLIOTECA NACIONAL

☎ 91 580 78 05; www.bne.es; Paseo de los Recoletos 20; admission free; ⌚ 10am-9pm Tue-Sat, 10am-2pm Sun; Ⓜ Colón

One of the most outstanding of the many grand edifices erected in the 19th century along the Paseo de los Recoletos, the 1892 Biblioteca Nacional (National Library) dominates the southern end of Plaza de Colón.

⊙ MUSEO ARQUEOLÓGICO NACIONAL

☎ 91 577 79 12; www.man.es, in Spanish; Calle de Serrano 13; admission free; ⌚ 9.30am-8pm Tue-Sat, 9.30am-3pm Sun & holidays; Ⓜ Serrano

Madrid's excellent archaeological museum will be undergoing major renovation works until well into 2011 and possibly beyond. In the meantime, small sections of the museum remain open on a revolving basis.

⊙ MUSEO DE LA ESCULTURA ABSTRACTA

www.munimadrid.es/museoairelibre/; Paseo de la Castellana; Ⓜ Rubén Darío

This fascinating open-air collection of 17 abstracts includes works by the renowned Basque artist Eduardo Chillida and the Catalan master Joan Miró, as well as Eusebio Sempere and Alberto Sánchez. The sculptures are beneath the overpass where Paseo de Eduardo Dato crosses Paseo de la Castellana.

⊙ MUSEO LÁZARO GALDIANO

☎ 91 561 60 84; www.flg.es, in Spanish; Calle de Serrano 122; adult/child/

WORTH THE TRIP

The **Plaza de Toros Monumental de Las Ventas** (Las Ventas; ☎ 91 556 92 37; www.las-ventas.com, in Spanish; Calle de Alcalá 237; ⌚ 9.30am-2.30pm Mon-Fri Oct-May, 9.30am-2.30pm Tue-Fri & 10am-1pm Sun Jun-Sep; Ⓜ Las Ventas) is the most important bullring in the world. Make it here in this classic example of the neo-Mudéjar style, and you've made it as a *torero* (bullfighter). Opened in 1931, it seats 25,000 spectators during the peak bullfighting season, which begins in May. The Museo Taurino has a collection of bullfighting paraphernalia. When you come up out of Las Ventas Metro station, the Plaza de Toros is there before you in all its glory.

Another temple to Madrid's sporting and cultural life, the **Estadio Santiago Bernabéu** (☎ 902 311 709; tickets 902 324 324; www.realmadrid.com; Calle de Concha Espina 1; self-guided tour adult/under 14 yr €15/10; ⌚ 10am-7pm Mon-Sat, 10.30am-6.30pm Sun, closed 5 hr before game; Ⓜ Santiago Bernabéu) is an essential stop for football fans visiting Madrid. For more information, see p20.

student & senior/€4/free/ 2; ⏱ 10am-4.30pm Wed-Mon; Ⓜ Gregorio Marañón

This imposing early-20th-century Italianate stone mansion, set just back from the street, houses the exceptional private collection of Don José Lázaro Galdiano (1862–1947). The 13,000 works of art and *objets d'art* (a quarter of which are on show at any time) include works by Van Eyck, Bosch, Zurbarán, Ribera, Goya, Claudio Coello, El Greco, Gainsborough and Constable. The ceiling in room 14 is a collage from some of Goya's more famous works.

🛍 SHOP

Shoppers will find their spiritual home in Salamanca. In addition to the places listed here, see p19 and p142 for more general information.

Outdoor art lives! Museo de la Escultura Abstracta

but exuberant adults will also find much to bring colour to their lives.

🛍 AMAYA ARZUAGA
Fashion & Shoes

☎ 91 426 28 15; www.amayaarzuaga .com; Calle de Lagasca 50; ⏱ 10.30am-8.30pm Mon-Sat; Ⓜ Velázquez

Sexy, bold and tastefully colourful, Amaya Arzuaga is one of Spain's most creative designers. The fusion of black with bright colours (think orange, red, fuchsia or turquoise) is very Spanish and oh-so-stylish.

🛍 AGATHA RUIZ DE LA PRADA *Fashion, Clothes & Shoes*

☎ 91 319 05 01; www.agatharuizde laprada.com; Calle de Serrano 27; ⏱ 10am-8.30pm Mon-Sat; Ⓜ Serrano

Crazy, candy-bright colours are the hallmark of this designer, who was one of the enduring cultural icons to emerge from Madrid's 1980s outpouring of creativity known as *la movida madrileña*. There's plenty of stuff for kids,

Agatha Ruiz de la Prada
Leading Spanish fashion designer (www.agatharuizdelaprada.com)

What do you like about Madrid? Madrid has very good vibrations. It's a very happy city and the people are some of the most open you'll find anywhere. You can make friends for your whole life quite easily. **What are your favourite restaurants?** When people come here they want the most typical like Lhardy (p76), Restaurante Sobrino de Botín (p51) or Casa Lucio (p64). They can be a little bit touristy, but Madrileños also like them. There are also super restaurants such as Zalacaín (p99). For tapas, Bocaito (p105). **What do you miss when you're not here?** I love the climate in Madrid. It makes you feel euphoric, it gives you lots of energy. **What's special about the people in Madrid?** Madrid is a city where we don't have anything. We don't have the sea etc. So we have to chase life.

✿ ARMAND BASI *Fashion & Shoes*
☎ 91 577 79 93; www.armandbasi.com; Calle de Claudio Coello 52; ⏱ 10am-8.30pm Mon-Sat; Ⓜ Serrano

Armand Basi is the purveyor of hip urban designs for the carefully casual (men and women). Just about anything you find here is well suited to a night out in Madrid, but especially the nightspots of Chueca and Salamanca.

✿ BOMBONERÍA SANTA *Chocolates*
☎ 91 576 86 46; Calle de Serrano 56; ⏱ 10am-3pm & 3.30-8.30pm Mon-Sat; Ⓜ Serrano

If your sense of style is as refined as your palate, the exquisite chocolates in this tiny shop are guaranteed to satisfy. They don't come cheap – a large box will cost at least €120!

✿ CAMPER *Fashion & Shoes*
☎ 91 578 25 60; www.camper.es; Calle de Serrano 24; ⏱ 9.30am-8.30pm Mon-Fri, to 9pm Sat; Ⓜ Serrano

The cool and quirky shoes of Camper are one of the great Spanish success stories. The designs are bowling-shoe chic with colourful, fun designs that are all about comfort.

✿ DAVIDELFÍN *Fashion*
☎ 91 700 04 53; www.davidelfin.es; Calle de Jorge Juan 31; ⏱ 10.30am-2.30pm & 4.30-8.30pm Mon-Sat; Ⓜ Velázquez

This young Spanish designer refuses to be pigeon-holed, with predominantly dark colours and military chic interspersed with surprising splashes of colour. If there's an overarching theme, it's casual, upmarket clothes with a rebellious spirit.

✿ DE VIAJE *Books & Travel*
☎ 91 577 98 99; www.deviaje.com, in Spanish; Calle de Serrano 41; ⏱ 10am-8.30pm Mon-Fri, 10.30am-2.30pm Sat; Ⓜ Serrano

The largest travel bookshop in Madrid, De Viaje has guidebooks, travel literature, travel gear and a travel agency with staff who know where to find what you're looking for.

✿ EKSEPTION & EKS *Fashion, Clothes & Shoes*
☎ 91 577 43 53; Calle de Velázquez 28; ⏱ 10.30am-2.30pm & 5-9pm Mon-Sat; Ⓜ Velázquez

The catwalklike entrance is the perfect introduction to brand names dedicated to urban chic with Balenciaga, Kokosalaki and Dries Van Noten in art-gallery-like displays; younger, more casual lines are next door.

STORM IN A D-CUP

In recent years Madrid's annual Pasarela Cibeles international fashion week has been steadily growing in importance, to the extent that it has surpassed Barcelona's fashion week and taken its place in the second tier of European fashion shows behind Paris and Milan. In 2006, however, the Pasarela Cibeles shot to international attention when the Spanish Association of Fashion Designers announced that excessively thin models would be banned from the catwalk. The new policy, which fuelled an international debate on the image presented by catwalk models, was adopted after protests by doctors and women's rights groups who argued that the models at last year's fashion show were unhealthily thin and set a bad example for young girls and women. The organisers of the Pasarela Cibeles proved true to their word in February 2007 when five out of the 69 female models were disqualified for having a body mass-to-height ratio, or Body Mass Index (BMI), of less than 18, a benchmark set by UN health experts. One of the rejected models had a BMI of just 16 – the equivalent of being 178cm tall (five feet 10 inches) and weighing just 50kg. Apart from some fashion shows in New York, no other fashion show has yet followed Madrid's lead. The French Couture Federation dismissed the new rules, saying that 'everyone would laugh' if Paris were to adopt the change. Organisers of Milan fashion week, however, promised to release a new code of conduct and have begun to hold plus-size shows to exhibit their support for Madrid's new policy.

GALLERY
Fashion & Accessories
☎ 91 576 79 31; www.gallerymadrid.com; Calle de Jorge Juan 38; 10.30am-8.30pm Mon-Sat; M Príncipe de Vergara or Velázquez
This stunning showpiece of men's fashions and accessories is the new Madrid in a nutshell – stylish, brand-conscious and all about having the right look. Expect brands such as Thom Browne and Raf Simons.

LOEWE *Fashion, Clothes & Shoes*
☎ 91 426 35 88; www.loewe.com; Calle de Serrano 34; 10am-8.30pm Mon-Sat; M Serrano

One of the classiest (and most expensive) Spanish labels, Loewe is the place to go for fine leather handbags and shoes and elegant fashions that are classical in inspiration and almost as pricey (and prestigious) as Louis Vuitton.

MANOLO BLAHNIK
Fashion & Shoes
☎ 91 575 96 48; www.manoloblahnik.com; Calle de Serrano 58; 10am-2pm & 4.30-8.30pm Mon-Sat; M Serrano
Nothing to wear to the Oscars? Do what many Hollywood celebrities do and head for Manolo Blahnik. The showroom is exclusive and each shoe is displayed like a work of art.

☐ MANTEQUERÍA BRAVO
Food Store
☎ 91 576 76 41; Calle de Ayala 24;
🕓 9.30am-2.30pm & 5.30-8.30pm
Mon-Fri, 9.30am-2.30pm Sat;
Ⓜ Serrano

Behind the attractive old façade lies a connoisseur's paradise, filled as it is with local cheeses, sausages, wines and coffees. They're great for a gift, but there's so much here that you won't want to share.

☐ PURIFICACIÓN GARCÍA
Fashion, Clothes & Shoes
☎ 91 576 72 76; www.purificaciongarcia.es, in Spanish; Calle de Serrano 92;
🕓 10am-8.30pm Mon-Sat; Ⓜ Serrano

Fashions may come and go but Puri consistently manages to keep ahead of the pack. Her signature style for men and women is elegant and mature designs that are just as at home in the workplace as at a wedding.

Golden mile of names, Calle de José Ortega y Gasset

AREA OF INTEREST – MADRID'S GOLDEN MILE

Salamanca may live for fashion, style and the ostentatious display of wealth that very much comes with the territory, but it's difficult to find a more exclusive stretch of fashion real estate anywhere in Europe than Calle de José Ortega y Gasset. If you stand close to the corner with Calle de Serrano, you'll be able to spot many of the great names of international fashion, among them Gucci, Cartier, Louis Vuitton, Dior and Burberry. Walk a little further west and you'll stumble upon Chanel, Dolce & Gabbana and Giorgio Armani. Known as *la milla del oro* (the golden mile), it's the starting point of many a shopper's love affair with Madrid and the perfect complement to the Spanish designers whose showrooms overflow from the streets to the south.

UNO DE 50 *Jewellery*

☎ 91 577 26 10; www.unode50.com, in Spanish; Calle de Ayala 26; ⏱ 10am-8.30pm Mon-Sat; Ⓜ Serrano
This innovative jewellery store offers up silver jewellery with only 50 produced of each design, and each displayed like a work of contemporary art.

VINÇON
Designer Homewares

☎ 91 578 05 20; www.vincon.com; Calle de Castelló 18; ⏱ 10am-8.30pm Mon-Sat; Ⓜ Príncipe de Vergara
Conceived in Barcelona when the city was Europe's centre of cool, Vinçon's presence in Madrid reflects the fact that the Spanish capital is fast becoming Barcelona's equal. Sleek, often fun and always cutting-edge homeware and all sorts of gadgets that you never knew you needed is what it's all about.

🍴 EAT

Although there are a few exceptions, eating in Salamanca is generally classy with a suitable price tag attached. In keeping with the barrio's seigneurial air, the atmosphere is less free-wheeling than in other Madrid barrios and, unusually for Madrid, dressing smartly is an unwritten rule. Fortunately, it's usually worth it.

AL-MOUNIA *Moroccan* €€

☎ 91 435 08 28; www.almounia.es, in Spanish; Calle de Recoletos 5; ⏱ 1.30-3.30pm & 9-11pm Mon-Sat; Ⓜ Colón
One of the longest-standing Moroccan restaurants promises the best couscous in town (it bears no relation to the couscous we all buy in a packet), subtly spiced lamb *tagines* (stews cooked in ceramic pots) and breathtaking hand-crafted traditional décor.

BIOTZA
Basque & Tapas €€

☎ 91 781 03 13; Calle de Claudio Coello 27; ⏱ 9am-midnight Mon-Thu, 9am-2am Fri & Sat; Ⓜ Serrano
Basque tapas *(pintxos)* and Madrid style make for a perfect marriage in this achingly cool Salamanca tapas bar. You could spend hours poring over (and translating) the menu, but the often surprising combination of tastes is a foody's dream.

EL ROCIO
Andalucian €€

☎ 91 431 24 45; www.restauranteel rocio.com, in Spanish; Calle de Don Ramón de la Cruz 28; ⏱ 1-4pm & 8.30-11.30pm Mon-Sat; Ⓜ Velázquez
Delicious rice dishes in all their glory, most of them laden with seafood, are what draw the crowds here. But the unifying theme is all things Andalucian,

from the decoration to the Mediterranean seafood, and fine steaks from southern Spain's interior.

🍴 LA CASA DEL ABUELO
Tapas   €€
☎ 902 027 334; Calle de Goya 57; ⏰ 8.30am-midnight; Ⓜ Goya

At the 'House of the Grandfather', the traditional order is a *chato* (small glass) of the heavy, sweet El Abuelo red wine and the heavenly *gambas a la plancha* (grilled prawns) or *gambas al ajillo* (prawns sizzling in garlic on little ceramic plates).

🍴 LA COLONIAL DE GOYA
Tapas   €€
☎ 91 575 63 06; Calle de Jorge Juan 34; ⏰ 8.30am-midnight Mon-Thu, 8.30am-1am Fri & Sat; Ⓜ Velázquez

This engaging little tapas bar all dressed in white serves dozens of different varieties of *pinchos* (tapas; from €3) with riffs on traditional Spanish recipes, as well as more hearty *raciones* (plate with tapas of similar variety), salads and carefully chosen wines. The chill-out music on the sound system and the dull roar of popularity only add to the charm.

Your *pintxos* (Basque tapas) addiction starts at Biotza

Wine, dine and shop fine at multitalented Sula (p100)

🍴 LA GALETTE
Vegetarian & European   €€

☎ 91 576 06 41; Calle del Conde de Aranda 11; ⏱ 2-5pm & 9pm-midnight Mon-Sat, 2-5pm Sun; Ⓜ Retiro; Ⓥ

Not everything in Salamanca is about the latest fashion. A delightfully intimate dining space, an extensive menu featuring dishes that largely adhere to the owner's philosophy of 'baroque vegetarian' and old-style service make for one of Salamanca's best restaurants.

🍴 LE CAFÉ *Spanish*   €€

☎ 91 781 15 86; Calle de los Recoletos 13; ⏱ lunch & dinner Mon-Sat, lunch only Sun; Ⓜ Retiro

It's almost impossible to get a table here on a weekday lunchtime when locals stream in from surrounding offices for the buzzy atmosphere, stylish but casual surrounds and good food: it's traditional Spanish fare (rice dishes are a recurring theme) with a few twists. Unlike other similar places, it's as popular as when it opened.

WORTH THE TRIP

Northern Madrid is home to some of the city's most exclusive restaurants. Among these is **Zalacaín** (☎ 91 561 48 40; www.restaurantezalacain.com; Calle de Álvarez de Baena 4; 1.15-4pm & 9pm-midnight Mon-Fri, 9pm-midnight Sat Sep-Jul; M Gregorio Marañón), a classy home to the best in traditional Basque or Navarran cooking. The pig's trotters filled with mustard and candied potato are a house speciality. The wine list (an estimated 35,000 bottles) is purported to be one of the best in the city and you should certainly dress to impress (men will need a tie). Don't expect change from €100 per person and don't be surprised if you see the king at the next table. From the Gregorio Marañón Metro station, walk northwest along the Paseo de la Castellana to the first major intersection, turn right on Calle de Maria de Molina, then take the first left. Zalacaín is 50m up the hill on your right.

🍽 MUMBAI MASSALA
Indian €€

☎ 91 435 71 94; www.mumbaimassala
.com; Calle de los Recoletos 14;
1.30-3.30pm & 9-11.30pm Sun-Thu,
1.30-3.30pm & 9pm-12.30am Fri & Sat;
M Retiro

Eating is a holistic experience at Mumbai Massala, where you can enjoy the full spectrum of South Indian curries and North Indian tandoori in stunningly decorated surrounds. Eating a butter chicken while perched (surprisingly comfortably) on an exquisite Indian swing chair is one of life's luxuries.

🍽 RAMSES LIFE & FOOD
Fusion & Spanish €€€

☎ 91 435 16 66; www.ramseslife.com;
Plaza de la Independencia 4; noon-
11.30pm; M Retiro

Opened in December 2007 and designed by Philippe Starck,

Ramses Life & Food is all the rage among Madrid's trendy, well-to-do set. The decoration is baroque and upmarket kitsch. Although the food gets mixed reviews it's worth experiencing this place at least once.

🍽 RESTAURANTE ESTAY
Tapas €€

☎ 91 578 04 70; www.estayrestaurante
.com; Calle de Hermosilla 46; 8am-
12.30am Mon-Sat; M Velázquez

Restaurante Estay is partly a standard Spanish bar where besuited waiters serve *café con leche* (white coffee) when they do breakfasts, and it's also partly a cool tapas bar known for its *pintxos* (Basque tapas; €2.90 to €4), which it calls 'haute cuisine in miniature', and international wines. It's all watched over by contemporary-art on the walls. It's an odd mix, but somehow it works.

🍴 SULA

Mediterranean Fusion €€€

☎ 91 781 61 97; www.sula.es; Calle de Jorge Juan 33; ⏰ restaurant 1.30-3.30pm & 8.30-11pm Mon-Sat, bar noon-11pm Mon-Wed, noon-11.30pm Thu-Sat; Ⓜ Velázquez

If you want to catch Salamanca's happening vibe, head for Sula, a gourmet food store, super-styl-ish tapas bar and clean-lined restaurant where Quique Dacosta (voted Spain's best chef in 2005) serves up a range of Mediterra-nean dishes that you won't find anywhere else. Design touches added by Amaya Arzuaga help to make this one of Madrid's coolest spaces. Rumour has it that David Beckham had one of his farewell parties here.

🍴 WAGABOO

Asian & Italian €€

☎ 91 578 33 68; www.wagaboo.com; Calle de Ayala 14; ⏰ 1.30-4pm & 8.30-11.30pm Sun-Thu, 1.30-4pm & 8.45pm-midnight Fri & Sat; Ⓜ Serrano

Fun eating is the motto of Waga-boo and this casual approach to life infuses every aspect of this place. Unlike many places in Sala-manca, you won't feel out of place if you dress down, and prices for the Italian- and Asian-influenced dishes offer respite from the usual Salamanca levels.

🍸 DRINK

🍸 CENTRO CUBANO DE ESPAÑA *Bar*

☎ 91 575 82 79; www.elcentrocubano.com; 1st fl, Calle de Claudio Coello 41; 1.30pm-2am Mon-Thu, 1.30pm-2.30am Fri & Sat, 1.30-5pm Sun; Ⓜ Serrano

Cubans from all over Madrid come here for *mojitos* (Cuban cocktails that taste just like they do back home), son-inflected (a Cuban music style) beats that transport them back to Havana and a dance floor welcoming anyone who has Latin rhythms in their soul.

🍸 EL LATERAL *Bar*

☎ 91 435 06 04; Calle de Velázquez 57; ⏰ noon-1am Sun-Thu, until late Fri & Sat; Ⓜ Velázquez or Nuñez de Balboa

This chic wine bar is cool in most of the right places, but it owes more to the old Salamanca of slick suits and classic wines than the new wave of style shaking up the barrio. Mind you, after a few drinks the crowd loosens up more than you'd think.

🍸 GEOGRAPHIC CLUB *Bar*

☎ 91 578 08 62; Calle de Alcalá 141; ⏰ 1pm-1.30am Sun-Wed, 1pm-2am Thu, 1pm-3am Fri & Sat; Ⓜ Retiro

With its elaborate stained-glass windows, ethno-chic from all over the world and laid-back at-

WORTH THE TRIP

Thai Gardens (☎ 91 577 88 84; www.thaigardensgroup.com; Paseo de la Habana 3; 2-4pm & 9pm-midnight Sun-Thu, 2-4pm & 9pm-1am Fri & Sat; M Nuevos Ministerios or Santiago Bernabéu) has moved from its famously verdant Salamanca home, but its followers have made the journey north en masse. The food is exquisite, and almost certainly the best Thai food on offer in Madrid. It attracts a classy clientele and the service is at once attentive and discreet. The decoration is modern yet littered with Thai antiques and plenty of greenery. Like many regulars, we feel that the atmosphere has lost something since it moved here, but you'll forget that as soon as you start eating.

mosphere, the Geographic Club is an excellent choice in Salamanca for an early-evening drink. We like the table built around an old hot-air balloon basket almost as much as the cavernlike pub downstairs.

★ PLAY

★ NIGHTCLUBS

★ ALMONTE
Flamenco Nightclub
☎ 91 563 25 04; Calle de Juan Bravo 35; 9.30pm-5am; M Nuñez de Balboa or Diego de León
If flamenco moves your feet as well as your soul, head to Almonte where the young and the beautiful crowd has the *sevillana* thing going on with the downstairs dance floor.

★ GARAMOND *Nightclub*
☎ 91 576 84 02; www.garamond.es, in Spanish; Calle de Claudio Coello 10; 10pm-5.30am; M Retiro
Garamond is very Salamanca, from its *puerta rigurosa* (strict dress entry policy) to a 30-plus crowd that has money to burn and likes to show it.

★ SPAS

★ CHI SPA *Spa*
☎ 91 578 13 40; www.thechispa.com; Calle del Conde de Aranda 6; 10am-9pm Mon-Fri, to 6pm Sat; M Retiro
Wrap up in a robe and slippers and prepare to be pampered in one of Europe's best day spas. Services include a massage (€65 per hour), facial (€55 to €95), body peeling (€60 to €90), manicure (€25) or pedicure (€35). Now what was it you were stressed about?

>CHUECA

Once down-at-heel, now gay-at-heart, Chueca could only happen in Madrid. The narrow streets of this supercool barrio (neighbourhood) tumble down the hill from Calle de Hortaleza and into the undisputed centre of Spanish gay culture.

Chueca is far more about doing than it is seeing, although its tangle of streets do have a certain raffish charm, a curious blend of Salamanca refinement and the proudly working-class origins of Malasaña. Chueca is dominated by one of Madrid's most visible subcultures and it has, not surprisingly, proved adept at speciality niches within the barrio itself. Calle de la Libertad is one of the best eating streets in Madrid, while Calle del Piamonte is an oasis of upmarket accessory shopping. Throw in a ceaseless buzz and some of the best nightlife in Madrid, and you'll quickly learn that Chueca has one of Madrid's most irresistible personalities.

One final thing: if you're not gay, don't be put off by the fact that Chueca is often described as being Madrid's gay capital. This is one of the capital's most inclusive districts.

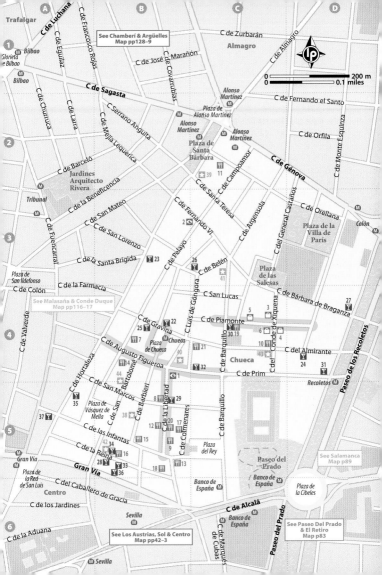

Trafalgar

A · B · C · D

1

C de Luchana
Glorieta de Bilbao
M Bilbao
M Bilbao
C de Eguilaz
C de Francisco Rojas

See Chamberí & Argüelles Map pp128–9

C de José de Marañón
C de Zurbarán
Almagro
C de Almagro

2

C de Churruca
C de Lara
C de Sagasta
C de Covarrubias
Alonso Martínez
C de Fernando el Santo
C de Meliá Lequerica
C de Serrano Anguita
Plaza de Alonso Martínez
M Alonso Martínez
M Alonso Martínez
C de Orfila
C de Monte Esquinza
C de Barceló
Jardines Arquitecto Rivera
Alonso Martínez
Plaza de Santa Bárbara
C de Génova

Tribunal
M

3

C de la Beneficencia
C de San Mateo
C de San Lorenzo
39
11
C de Campoamor
C de Santa Teresa
C de Orellana
C de Génova
C del General Castaños
C de Orellana
Plaza de la Villa de París
Colón
M
Colón

C de Fuencarral
C de la Santa Brígida
C de Pelayo
2
C de Fernando VI
C de Argensola
23
26
C de Belén
41
C San Lucas
Plaza de las Salesas

Plaza de San Ildefonso
C de Colón
C de la Farmacia

See Malasaña & Conde Duque Map pp116–17

C de Luis de Góngora
C de Bárbara de Braganza
27

4

C de Valverde
C de Gravina
22
25
Chueca
M
21
90
C de Piamonte
5
3
30 19
6
10
4
C del Almirante
C de Xiquena
24
31
Plaza de Chueca
C de Augusto Figueroa
32
C de Prim
Chueca
Recoletos
M
Paseo de los Recoletos

C de Hortaleza
C de San Bartolomé
44
1
C de Barquillo
C de Barquillo

5

C de Valverde
35
C de San Marcos
Plaza de Vázquez de Mella
38
C de Barbieri
C de la Libertad
29
12
17
20
15
9
Plaza del Rey
37
C de las Infantas
34
43
16
28
33
36
18
13
C de Colmenares
Banco de España
Banco de España

See Salamanca Map p89

Paseo del Prado

6

M Gran Vía
Plaza de la Red de San Luis
Gran Vía
C del Caballero de Gracia
Gran Vía
Centro
C de los Jardines
M Sevilla
C de la Reina
Sevilla
C de Aduana
Plaza de la Cibeles
M Sevilla

See Los Austrias, Sol & Centro Map pp42–3

C de Alcalá
Banco de España
C del Marqués de Cubas
Paseo del Prado

See Paseo Del Prado & El Retiro Map p83

N
0 ___ 200 m
0 ___ 0.1 miles

SEE

GALERÍA MORIARTY

☎ 91 531 43 65; www.galeriamoriarty
.com; Calle de la Libertad 22; admission
free; ⏰ 11am-2pm & 5-8.30pm Tue-Sat;
Ⓜ Chueca

You know a street has the
ultimate mark of approval when
Galería Moriarty moves in. One
of the cultural focal points of *la
movida madrileña* in the 1980s,
it still draws a cutting-edge
catalogue of international and
local artists.

SOCIEDAD GENERAL DE AUTORES Y EDITORES

www.sgae.es; Calle de Fernando VI 4;
Ⓜ Alonso Martínez

Madrid's sole answer to Gaudí's
Barcelona, this swirling, melting
wedding cake of a building is a
joyously self-indulgent ode to
modernismo. It only opens to the
public on the first Monday of October (International Architecture
Day), but it's far more impressive
from the street.

SHOP

IÑAKI SAMPEDRO
Handbags & Accessories

☎ 91 319 45 65; www.inakisampedro
.com, in Spanish; Calle del Conde de
Xiquena 13; ⏰ 10.30am-2pm & 5-
8.30pm Mon-Sat; Ⓜ Chueca or Colón

Arguably Spain's most colourful and innovative collection of
hand-painted handbags and other
accessories are available at this
wonderful little shop. They're not
cheap, but are unmistakably Spanish and superstylish.

LURDES BERGADA *Fashion*

☎ 91 531 99 58; Calle del Conde de
Xiquena 8; ⏰ 10.30am-8.30pm Mon-Sat;
Ⓜ Chueca or Colón

Classy and original men's and
women's fashions are the work
of this mother-son designer team
from Barcelona. It's stylish in a very
Chueca kind-of-way.

MARTEL KEE *Fashion*

☎ 91 319 86 11; Calle de Piamonte 15;
⏰ 11am-2.30pm & 3-9pm Mon-Sat;
Ⓜ Chueca

It's a strange fact of Spanish life that
French Connection has yet to open
its own store in Spain. Until it does,
head to this small boutique, which
also has other stylishly casual lines.

PIAMONTE *Fashion & Shoes*

☎ 91 523 07 66; www.piamonteshop
.com, in Spanish; Calle de Piamonte 16;
⏰ 10.30am-8.30pm Mon-Fri, 11am-
8.30pm Sat; Ⓜ Chueca

One of the favourite shoe shops
of Madrileñas looking for that
special something for an important
occasion. This is one of the major
standard-bearers for Chueca's
sense of style.

🍴 EAT

If you could choose just one barrio for eating out, Chueca would be a leading candidate. And if you could choose just one street, Calle de la Libertad would probably take the prize. Chueca's secret is stylish dining with a creative, artsy vibe but without the Salamanca price tag.

🍴 BACO Y BETO *Tapas* €€
☎ 91 522 84 81; www.bacoybeto.com, in Spanish; Calle de Pelayo 24; 🕑 8pm-1am Mon-Fri, 2-4pm & 8pm-1am Sat; Ⓜ Chueca

Friends in Madrid begged us not to include this place and we *were* tempted to keep it all to ourselves. Why? Baco y Beto serves up some of the tastiest tapas in Madrid.

🍴 BAZAAR *Mediterranean & Nouvelle Cuisine* €€
☎ 91 523 39 05; www.restaurantbazaar .com ; Calle de la Libertad 21; 🕑 1.15-4pm & 8.30-11.45pm; Ⓜ Chueca

With fresh tastes, hardwood floors, grand windows, theatre lighting and comfy leather seats, Bazaar has drawn an 'in' crowd for quite a while and its popularity shows no sign of waning. It doesn't take reservations so arrive early.

🍴 BOCAITO *Tapas* €€
☎ 91 532 12 19; www.bocaito.com; Calle de la Libertad 4-6; 🕑 Mon-Fri & Sat evenings; Ⓜ Chueca or Banco de España

Film-maker Pedro Almodóvar finds this bar and restaurant in the traditional Madrid style 'the best antidepressant'. Forget about the sit-down restaurant and just jam into the bar, order a few *raciones* (plate with tapas of the same variety) off the menu, wash them down with a gritty red and enjoy the theatre in which these busy barmen excel.

🍴 BOGA BAR *Seafood & Rice Dishes* €€€
☎ 91 532 18 50; Calle del Almirante 11; 🕑 1.30-4pm & 9pm-midnight Mon-Sat, 1.30-4pm Sun; Ⓜ Chueca

Boga Bar is right at home in this select corner of Madrid and its seafood is among the freshest in the city. The desserts are also wonderful.

🍴 CACAO SAMPAKA *Food Store* €
☎ 91 319 58 40; www.cacaosampaka .com; Calle de Orellana 4; 🕑 10am-9.30pm; Ⓜ Alonso Martínez; ♿

If you thought chocolate was simply all about fruit 'n' nut, think again. This gourmet chocolate shop is a chocoholic's dream-come-true, with more combinations to go with humble cocoa than you ever imagined possible. The attached café serves breakfasts and great coffee, light lunches and cakes.

🍽 CIRCUS *Noodle Bar* €

☎ 91 522 52 15; Calle de la Libertad 13; ⏱ 1-5pm & 9pm-12.30am Mon-Sat, 1-4.30pm Sun; Ⓜ Chueca; Ⓥ 🚻

If you like to linger over your meal, look elsewhere, but for those of you who enjoy your noodles with plenty of coconut milk and lime juice, this place is excellent. Stylish but fresh and cheerful, it revels in its slightly offbeat motto of 'Very Fashion Fast Food'.

🍽 EL ORIGINAL
Spanish €€

☎ 91 522 90 69; www.eloriginal.es, in Spanish; Calle de las Infantas 44; ⏱ 1.30-4pm & 9-11.30pm Mon-Sat; Ⓜ Chueca or Banco de España

With the best products and signature dishes from each of the regions of Spain, you might expect El Original to be a bastion of traditionalism. Then you roll up and find trees growing in the sleek-lined dining room. Prices are reasonable, another reason why we hope this place lasts the distance.

🍽 GASTROMAQUIA
Tapas €€

☎ 91 522 64 13; Calle de Pelayo 8; ⏱ 1.30-5pm Mon, 1.30-5pm & 9pm-12.30am Tue-Thu & Sat, 9pm-12.30am Fri; Ⓜ Chueca

Gastromaquia, overseen by renowned chef Ivan Sánchez, encourages Spaniards to relearn eating habits, offering an international journey into what he calls 'universal tapas'.

🍽 ISOLÉE *Food Store & Café* €€

☎ 902 876 136; www.isolee.com; Calle de las Infantas 19; ⏱ 10am-10pm Mon-Thu, 10am-1am Fri & Sat, 4-10pm Sun; Ⓜ Gran Vía or Chueca; 🚻

Multipurpose lifestyle stores are all the rage in Madrid and there's none more stylish than Isolée. It sells a range of everything from clothes and shoes to CDs and food. The minimalist café is dressed in white and perfect for a coffee and cake or something more substantial such as pasta, wok dishes and salads.

🍽 JANATOMO *Japanese* €€

☎ 91 521 55 66; Calle de la Reina 27; ⏱ 1.30-4.30pm & 8.30pm-midnight Tue-Sun; Ⓜ Gran Vía

Having undergone a style overhaul, Janatomo has added a Zen ambience to its splendid Japanese cooking. The sight of tour groups from the home country piling in is all the confirmation we need.

🍽 KIM BU MBU *African* €€

☎ 91 521 26 81; Calle de Colmenares 7; ⏱ 1.30-4pm & 9pm-midnight Mon-Sat, 1.30-4.30pm Sun; Ⓜ Chueca or Banco de España

With stunning African décor, Kim Bu Mbu is the best place in Madrid to get acquainted with the perhaps unfamiliar Senegalese, and other unusual tastes from around Africa.

🍽 LA PAELLA DE LA REINA
Rice Dishes €€

☎ 91 531 18 85; www.lapaelladelareina .com, in Spanish; Calle de la Reina 39; ⏱ 1-4pm & 8pm-midnight; Ⓜ Banco de España

This is one of Madrid's better paella restaurants and, as is the custom, you need two people to make an order. The typical Valencia paella is cooked with beans, chicken and rabbit, but there are plenty of seafood varieties on offer.

🍽 MAISON BLANCHE
Food Store €€

☎ 91 522 82 17; Calle de Piamonte 10; ⏱ 9am-12.30am Mon-Sat, noon-6pm Sun; Ⓜ Chueca

If you have a friend from Barcelona who's too-cool-for-Madrid, bring them here and they might just change their mind. A gourmet food store and stylish café, this has become one of the most fashionable places in town for A-list celebrities. This is the new Madrid and it's very cool. There's live jazz from 2.30pm to 4.30pm Saturday.'

🍽 RESTAURANTE MOMO
Spanish €€

☎ 91 532 73 48; Calle de Libertad 8; ⏱ 1-4pm & 8.30pm-midnight Mon-Sat; Ⓜ Chueca

Momo is a Chueca beacon of reasonably priced home-cooking for a casual but stylish crowd. It's got an artsy vibe and is ideal for those who want a hearty meal without too much elaboration. The *menú del día* (fixed-price three-course meal) is one of Madrid's bargains and the famous chocolate *moco* (snot) is the tastiest of dessert dishes despite its worrying name.

🍽 WAGABOO
Asian & Italian €€

☎ 91 531 65 67; www.wagaboo.com, in Spanish; Calle de Gravina 18; ⏱ 1-4pm & 8.30-11.30pm Sun-Thu, 1.30-4pm & 8.45pm-midnight Fri & Sat; Ⓜ Chueca

Wagaboo offers well-priced pasta and Asian noodle dishes with some surprising combinations. It's wildly popular for both lunch and dinner, so either make a reservation or be prepared to wait.

🍸 DRINK

Chueca overflows with quintessentially Madrid watering holes, spanning the full range from old *tabernas* to chichi new places where style is everything.

🍸 ANTIGUA CASA ÁNGEL SIERRA
Taberna

☎ 91 531 01 26; Calle de Gravina 11; ⏱ 12.30pm-1am; Ⓜ Chueca

This historic old *taberna* (tavern) is the antithesis of modern Chueca chic. It has hardly changed since it opened in 1917 and thankfully that includes the wonderful façade. Fronting onto the Plaza de Chueca, it can get pretty lively of an evening.

▼ AREIA *Lounge Bar*
☎ 91 310 03 07; www.areiachillout .com, in Spanish; Calle de la Hortaleza 92; ⌚ 1pm-3am; Ⓜ Chueca
The ultimate lounge bar by day (cushions and chill-out music abound), Areia is equally enjoyable by night when DJs take over with deep and chill House, nu jazz, bossa and electronica. It's cool, funky and low-key all at once.

▼ BRISTOL BAR *Café-Bar*
☎ 91 522 45 68; www.bristolbar .es; Calle del Almirante 20; ⌚ 10am-12.30am Mon-Wed, 10am-2am Thu & Fri, 11am-2am Sat; Ⓜ Gran Vía
You could come here for the English breakfast (€13) or the brunch (€21), but we like this place for its 75 different types of gin. The atmosphere is that of a quiet café by day, a sophisticated gin parlour after sunset.

▼ CAFÉ ACUARELA *Bar*
☎ 91 522 21 43; Calle de Gravina 10; ⌚ 11am-2am Sun-Thu, to 3am Fri & Sat; Ⓜ Chueca
Right on Plaza de Chueca and long a centrepiece of gay Madrid, this is an agreeable, dimly lit

---

MADRID'S BEST TERRAZAS
One of the pleasures of Madrid when the weather's fine is the proliferation of bars and restaurants with *terrazas* (outdoor tables), a Madrid favourite whether for breakfast or a late-night *copa* (drink).
> Plaza de Santa Ana, Huertas
> Plaza de Oriente, Los Austrias
> Café-Restaurante El Espejo (below)
> Plaza de la Paja, La Latina
> Plaza de Olavide, Chamberí
> Hotel de las Letras, Gran Vía 11

salon for quiet conversation or for more *marcha* (action) as the night gears up.

▼ CAFÉ BELÉN *Bar*
☎ 91 308 27 47; Calle de Belén 5; ⌚ 3.30pm-3am; Ⓜ Chueca
Café Belén is cool in all the right places: lounge and chill-out music, dim lighting, a great range of drinks – the *mojitos* (Cuban cocktails) are among the best in Madrid – and a low-key crowd.

▼ CAFÉ-RESTAURANTE EL ESPEJO *Café-Bar*
☎ 91 308 23 47; www.restaurante elespejo.com, in Spanish; Paseo de los Recoletos 3; ⌚ 8am-2am; Ⓜ Colón
This was once a haunt of writers and intellectuals, and it's easy to be a little overwhelmed by all the mirrors, chandeliers and discreet charm of another era. What

changes all that is that the outdoor tables are some of Madrid's most popular drinking *terrazas* on a warm summer's evening.

▼ DEL DIEGO *Cocktail Bar*
☎ 91 523 31 06; Calle de la Reina 12; ⏰ 7pm-3am Mon-Thu, to 3.30am Fri & Sat; Ⓜ Gran Vía

A vaguely old-world café-style ambience pervades Del Diego, but you can hear yourself talk and the cocktails (mostly around €9) are among the best in the barrio.

▼ DIURNO *Café*
☎ 91 522 00 09; www.diurno.com, in Spanish; Calle de San Marcos 37; ⏰ 10am-midnight Mon-Thu, 10am-1am Fri, 11am-1am Sat, 11am-midnight Sun; Ⓜ Chueca

It's not often that we recommend DVD stores in our guidebooks, but the attached café is always full with a fun Chueca crowd relaxing amid the ample greenery. We recommend that you join them because this has become one of the most laid-back centres of barrio life.

Wise men and women relax at Café Belén

V

BARRIOS

CHUECA

☏ EL CLANDESTINO *Bar*
☎ 91 521 55 63; Calle de Barquillo 34; ⏱ 8pm-3am; Ⓜ Chueca

We've been wandering around Madrid for years and this is one bar we always find full. What it's doing right is a low-key atmosphere, funky (and occasionally live indie rock) music and good *mojitos*.

☏ GRAN CAFÉ DE GIJÓN *Café-Bar*
☎ 91 521 54 25; www.cafegijon.com; Paseo de los Recoletos 21; ⏱ 7am-1.30am; Ⓜ Chueca or Banco de España

This graceful old café has been serving coffee, meals and pricey drinks since 1888 and has long been a favourite with Madrid's literati.

☏ LA BARDEMCILLA *Bar*
☎ 91 521 42 56; Calle de Augusto Figueroa 47; ⏱ noon-5.30pm & 8pm-2am Mon-Fri, 8pm-2am Sat; Ⓜ Chueca

Run by the family of film heartthrob Javier Bardem, this bar has an agreeable buzz most nights of the week. A comfortable space to relax, a slightly bohemian air and a loyal following add up to a great package.

☏ LE COCK *Bar*
☎ 91 532 28 26; Calle de la Reina 16; ⏱ 8pm-3am Mon-Thu, to 3.30am Fri & Sat; Ⓜ Gran Vía

The décor that resembles an old gentleman's club notwithstanding, the Cock gets lively on weekends when the tables all seem to be reserved. That's probably because it's a popular weekend haunt of A-listers and a refined 30-something crowd.

☏ LIBERTAD 8 *Bar*
☎ 91 532 11 50; www.libertad8cafe.es, in Spanish; Calle de la Libertad 8; ⏱ 4pm-2.30am Mon-Thu, 4pm-3am Fri & Sat; Ⓜ Chueca

Here's a novelty you won't find elsewhere – at 9pm many nights a storyteller does his or her stuff, often role-playing into the bargain. The audience in this tiled old Spanish bar love to get involved and usually stay on for drinks afterwards.

☏ LOLA BAR *Lounge Bar*
☎ 91 522 34 83; www.lola-bar.com; Calle de la Reina 25; ⏱ 6pm-3am Tue-Sat; Ⓜ Gran Vía

If you like your music chilled-out, Lola Bar is a great place to start your night. On weekends the DJ ups the tempo a little, but it's more lounge than House and you may find yourself staying longer than you planned. Our only complaint is that *mojitos* are a steep €8.50.

Lola Moriarty
Director, Galería Moriarty (www.galeriamoriarty.com, in Spanish)

What do you remember about la movida madrileña? Back then, we had no sense of the future. **Has that changed?** We've all grown older and the spirit of the time changes. But we still like to find the next new thing and do it with style. **What do you love about Chueca?** The gay community has converted Chueca into one of the most stylish barrios in Madrid. But more than that, Chueca is a young barrio that's very alive – it's here that you find the pulse of the city. **What's special about Madrid?** Madrid is a very modern and a very open city. No one is from Madrid and there's no sense of nationalism. It's also a very permissive city with endless energy. **Can you sum up Madrid in one sentence?** Madrid opens its arms, but never closes them.

▼ MAMÁ INÉS *Café*

☎ 91 523 23 33; www.mamaines.com, in Spanish; Calle de la Hortaleza 22; ⏱ 10am-2am Sun-Thu, to 3.30am Fri & Sat; Ⓜ Chueca

A gay male meeting place with its low lights and low music, this café-bar is never sleazy and has a laid-back ambience by day and a romantic air by night. By day you can get breakfast, yummy pastries and all the gossip on where that night's hot spot will be.

▼ MUSEO CHICOTE *Cocktail Bar*

☎ 91 532 67 37; www.museo-chicote .com; Gran Vía 12; ⏱ 6pm-4am Mon-Sat; Ⓜ Gran Vía

The founder of this Madrid landmark is said to have invented more than a hundred cocktails (it claims its Cuban *mojitos* are Madrid's finest), which the likes of Hemingway, Sophia Loren and Frank Sinatra have all enjoyed at one time or another. It's still frequented by film stars and top socialites and it's at its best after midnight when a lounge atmosphere takes over, couples cuddle on the curved benches and some of the city's best DJs do their stuff (CDs are available).

▼ STOP MADRID *Bar*

☎ 91 521 88 87; Calle de la Hortaleza 11; ⏱ 12.30-4pm & 6.30pm-2am; Ⓜ Gran Vía

This terrific old *taberna* is friendly, invariably packed with people and wins the vote of at least one Lonely Planet author for the best sangria in Madrid.

⭐ PLAY

Chueca is one of those barrios where you simply have to follow the crowds coursing through the narrow streets on weekends in order to find the latest 'in' nightclub.

⭐ LIVE MUSIC

▣ EL JUNCO JAZZ CLUB *Jazz*

☎ 91 319 20 81; www.eljunco.com; Plaza de Santa Bárbara 10; admission free; ⏱ 11pm-6am; Ⓜ Alonso Martínez

Night owls who are tired of the House music that pervades so many of Madrid clubs will love the nightly live jazz concerts, followed by DJs spinning funk, nu jazz and innovative groove beats. The emphasis is on black music and the crowd is classy and casual.

⭐ NIGHTCLUBS

▣ CLUB 54 STUDIO *Nightclub*

www.studio54madrid.com, in Spanish; Calle de Barbieri 7; ⏱ 11.30pm-6am Thu-Sat; Ⓜ Chueca

Modelled on the famous New York club Studio 54, this nightclub draws a predominantly gay crowd, but its target market (and door policy) is more upmarket than many in the barrio.

⭐ LOCAL CAFÉ BAR LOUNGE
Café & Nightclub

☎ 91 532 76 10; www.barlocalchueca .com, in Spanish; Calle de la Libertad 28; ⏰ 5pm-3am; Ⓜ Chueca

With its swirling colour scheme, funky soul, disco and deep House beats and a predominantly gay crowd, Local is Chueca in a nutshell.

⭐ SUSAN CLUB *Nightclub*

Calle de la Reina 23; ⏰ 8.30pm-3am Tue-Sat; Ⓜ Gran Vía

It's hard to know what sort of music you'll find at the cosy little Susan Club, because the bar staff readily admit that they play whatever suits their mood. As a general rule, it's quite funky and down-tempo early in the night with more frenetic and popular tunes as the crowd starts to sweat.

⭐ VERVET *Nightclub*

☎ 91 521 73 79; Calle del Almirante 12; ⏰ 11pm-3am Wed-Sun; Ⓜ Chueca

If you could bottle the energy of Chueca with the sophistication of Salamanca, you'd end up with Vervet. The cocktails are first-rate and there seems to be a door

policy of only admitting the beautiful people of Madrid. Café Olivier is the attached restaurant.

⭐ WHY NOT? *Nightclub*

Calle de San Bartolomé 7; ⏰ 10.30pm-late; Ⓜ Chueca

Narrow and packed with bodies, gay-friendly Why Not? is the sort of place where nothing's left to the imagination (the gay and straight crowd that come here are pretty amorous) and it's full nearly every night of the week. Pop and top 40s music are the standard here, and the dancing crowd is mixed and is as serious about having a good time as it is about heavy petting.

⭐ SPAS

⭐ SPA RELAJARSE *Spa*

☎ 91 308 61 48; www.sparelajarse.es, in Spanish; Calle de Barquillo 43; ⏰ 11am-11pm Mon-Sat, 1-9pm Sun; Ⓜ Chueca

Step inside this intimate little spa and you can't help but feel relaxed. With a range of options (the Especial Spa includes a hydro-massage pool with strawberries and Möet Chandon for €170 per couple, while the Especial Spa with a 'romantic dinner' costs €260 for two), this may be one for a special occasion.

>MALASAÑA & CONDE DUQUE

Malasaña was the birthplace of *la movida madrileña* (sociocultural movement following Francisco Franco's death) in the early 1980s and it has never really shaken off its reputation for hedonistic nightlife and a funky beat. Ageing rockers rub shoulders with cool urban professionals while teenage wannabes course through the streets in large groups. It's about bars promising music heavy on the electric guitar or drums, and hip restaurants with chill-out tunes to accompany your meal. Quirky shops are another feature, for this is Madrid's home of casual-but-cool street wear. The Glorieta de Bilbao in the north is the gateway, Calle de Manuela Malasaña is an emblematic Madrid restaurant street, and down the hill towards the Plaza del Dos de Mayo is where the action really starts as the sun sets. The area is not without its problems, although this is largely restricted to the small, seedy red-light zone immediately north of Gran Vía.

Conde Duque is much quieter, but it's the sort of barrio (neighbourhood) that is drawing a small but devoted following of locals-in-the-know to its cosy bars and the occasional top restaurant.

MALASAÑA & CONDE DUQUE

Please see over for map

👁 SEE
👁 MUSEO MUNICIPAL

☎ 91 588 86 72; www.munimadrid.es
/museomunicipal; Calle de Fuencarral 78;
Ⓜ Tribunal; ♿

The elaborate and restored baroque entrance, raised in 1721 by Pedro de Ribera, opens onto this excellent museum which charts the historical evolution of Madrid. The highlights include paintings by Goya, while Madrid de los Austrias (Habsburg Madrid) is brought to life with an absorbing model of 1830s Madrid. The museum is currently closed for major renovations and is slated to reopen sometime in 2010.

👁 MUSEO MUNICIPAL DE ARTE CONTEMPORÁNEO

☎ 91 588 59 28; www.munimadrid
.es/museoartecontemporaneo; Calle
del Conde Duque 9-11; admission free;
🕒 10am-2pm & 5.30-9pm Tue-Sat,
10.30am-2.30pm Sun & holidays;
Ⓜ Noviciado or San Bernardo; ♿

Spread over two floors, this rich collection (mostly paintings, along with some photography) showcases Spanish art from the 1920s until the present.

🛍 SHOP

Wander around Malasaña and, to a lesser extent, Conde Duque and you'll quickly discover that this is a barrio with attitude. It's a place to wander in search of offbeat clothing stores, that tattoo parlour you've been looking for and hair stylists capable of doing things you never imagined.

🛍 ADOLFO DOMINGUEZ
Fashion, Clothes & Shoes

☎ 91 523 39 38; www.adolfodoming
uez.com, in Spanish; Calle de Fuencarral
5; 🕒 10am-9pm Mon-Sat; Ⓜ Gran Vía

The stylish shop of this inventive Spanish designer is where you'll find utterly casual and colourful designs for the consciously cool among us.

🛍 CUSTO BARCELONA
Fashion, Clothes & Shoes

☎ 91 360 46 36; www.custo-barcelona
.com; Calle de Fuencarral 29; 🕒 10am-
9pm Mon-Sat, noon-8pm Sun; Ⓜ Gran Vía

The chic shop of Barcelona designer Custo Dalmau wears its Calle de Fuencarral address well, because the now-iconic T-shirts are at once edgy, awash in attitude and artfully displayed. It's not to everyone's taste, but always worth a look.

🛍 DIVINA PROVIDENCIA
Fashion, Clothes & Shoes

☎ 91 521 10 95; www.divinaproviden
cia.com, in Spanish; Calle de Fuencarral
45; 🕒 11am-9pm Mon-Sat; Ⓜ Gran Vía
or Tribunal

Divina Providencia has moved seamlessly from fresh new face

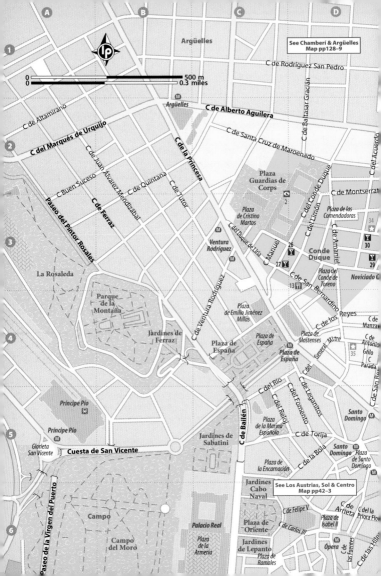

See Chamberí & Argüelles
Map pp128–9

C de Rodríguez San Pedro

C de Alberto Aguilera

C de Altamirano

Argüelles

C de Baltasar Gracián

C del Marqués de Urquijo

C de Santa Cruz de Marcenado

C de la Princesa

C del Acuerdo

C de Juan Álvarez Mendizábal

C de Quintana

C de Tutor

C de Buen Suceso

Plaza
Guardias de
Corps

C del Conde Duque

C de Montserrat

Paseo del Pintor Rosales

C de Ferraz

Plaza de
Cristino
Martos

C Manuel

C de Limón

Plaza de las
Comendadoras

C de Amaniel

Ventura
Rodríguez

C del Duque de Liria

26

27

Conde
Duque

30

29

La Rosaleda

C de San Bernardino

C del Conde de
Toreno

Noviciado

Parque
de la
Montaña

C de Ventura Rodríguez

Plaza
de Emilio Jiménez
Millas

13

C de los Reyes

C de
Manza

Jardines de
Ferraz

Plaza de
España

Plaza de
Mostenses

Plaza de

Mitre

C de
Antonio
Grilo

Plaza de
España

C del

General

C de San

C de
Parada

35

Plaza de
España

C del Río

C del Fomento

C de Leganitos

Santo
Domingo

Príncipe Pío

C de Bailén

C del Reloj

Príncipe Pío

Plaza de
la Marina
Española

C de Torija

C de la Bola

Santo
Domingo

Glorieta
San Vicente

Cuesta de San Vicente

Jardines de
Sabatini

Plaza de
Santo
Domingo

Plaza de
la Encarnación

Paseo de la Virgen del Puerto

Jardines
Cabo
Naval

See Los Austrias, Sol & Centro
Map pp42–3

C de la
Priora Flo

Campo

C de Felipe V

Plaza de
Isabel II

C de
Arrieta

Palacio Real

Plaza de
Oriente

C de Carlos III

Ópera

C de las Fuentes

C de las Hile

Campo
del Moro

Plaza
de la
Armería

Jardines
de Lepanto

Plaza de
Ramales

0   500 m
0   0.3 miles

on the Madrid fashion scene to almost mainstream stylish, with fun clothes for women and strong retro and Asian influences.

🏬 MERCADO DE FUENCARRAL
Fashion, Clothes & Accessories

☎ 91 521 41 52; www.mdf.es/Madrid, in Spanish; Calle de Fuencarral 45; ⏰ 11am-9pm Mon-Sat; Ⓜ Tribunal
Threatened with closure, saved by popular demand, the dozens of small shops here are Madrid's home of alternative club-cool. This place revels in its reverse snobbery, and it's funky, grungy and filled to the rafters with torn T-shirts and more black leather and studs than you'll ever need.

🏬 PATRIMONIO COMUNAL OLIVERO *Olive Oil*

☎ 91 308 05 05; www.pco.es, in Spanish; Calle de Mejía Lequerica 1; ⏰ 10am-2pm & 5-8pm Mon-Fri, 10am-2pm Sat, closed Aug; Ⓜ Alonso Martínez
Spain is the world's largest producer of olive oils, and some of the best from all over Spain are to be found here. Those from Andalucía have the best reputation, but for a wide sampling why not try the box of 10 mini bottles for just €8?

🏬 SNAPO *Alternative Fashion*

☎ 91 532 12 23; snapo@wanadoo.es; Calle del Espíritu Santo 5; ⏰ 11am-2pm & 5-8.30pm Mon-Sat; Ⓜ Tribunal

You wouldn't find Snapo anywhere but in Malasaña, with edgy street wear that typifies the barrio's rebellious spirit. Imagine a T-shirt of Pope John Paul II with fist raised and 'Vatican 666' emblazoned across the front and you get the idea.

🍴 EAT

For such a retro barrio, Malasaña does a surprising range in high-quality fusion restaurants that draw a hip, 30-something crowd. If sleek surrounds and creative cooking are your thing, Malasaña's your place. If not, there are plenty of other places to draw you here.

🍴 A DOS VELAS *Fusion*   €€

☎ 91 446 18 63; www.adosvelas .net, in Spanish; Calle de San Vicente Ferrer 16; ⏰ 1.30-5pm & 8.30pm-1am; Ⓜ Tribunal; ♿ ♨
We love this place and Madrid's discerning restaurant public clearly agrees. The food is always creative, with Mediterranean cooking fused with occasional Indian or even Argentinian flavours, a lovely dining area with soft lighting and exposed brick, and service that's attentive without being intrusive.

🍴 BODEGA DE LA ARDOSA
Tapas   €€

☎ 91 521 49 79; Calle de Colón 13; ⏰ 8am-1.30am Sun-Thu, to 2.30am Fri & Sat; Ⓜ Tribunal; ♿ ♨

Drink up the outdoor buzz at Plaza del Dos de Mayo

Going strong since 1892, the charming, wood-panelled bar of Bodega de la Ardosa could equally be recommended as a favourite Malasaña drinking hole. Then again, to come here and not try the *salmorejo* (soup based on tomato and bread) would be a crime. On weekend nights, there's scarcely room to move.

🍴 CASA DO COMPAÑEIRO
Galician & Tapas €€
☎ 91 521 57 02; Calle de San Vicente Ferrer 44; ⏲ 1.30pm-2am; Ⓜ Tribunal
Tucked away in the streets just up from Plaza del Dos de Mayo, this old Madrid *taberna* (tavern) has a wonderful tiled-and-wood

façade, basic wooden stools, marble-top tables and terrific tapas from Galicia.

🍴 COMO ME LO COMO
Spanish & International Fusion €€
☎ 91 523 13 23; Calle de Andrés Borrego 16; ⏲ 1-4.30pm & 9pm-1am Mon-Sat; Ⓜ Noviciado
Traditional Spanish dishes given the odd international twist to suit 21st-century palates and excellent value for money are the hallmarks of this trendy place down Malasaña's lower end. Portions are generous and the friendly service is another winner, as is the three-course evening menu for €16.90.

MALASAÑA & CONDE DUQUE > EAT

MALASAÑA & CONDE DUQUE

🍴 CON DOS FOGONES
International   €€

☎ 91 559 63 26; www.condosfogones
.com, in Spanish; Calle de San Bernardino
9; ⏱ 1-5pm & 8.30pm-1am; Ⓜ Plaza de
España; ♿ 👶

Con Dos Fogones is cool and
classy, with bright colours softly lit
by designer lamps, and the food
is everything from splendid salads
and quality hamburgers to great
slabs of fine Argentinian beef.
There's quite a buzz about this
place at the moment, but we think
it will last the distance.

🍴 CONACHE
Mediterranean   €€

☎ 91 522 95 00; Plaza de San Ildefonso; ⏱ 9.30am-1.30am Mon-Thu,
9.30am-2.30am Fri & Sat, 7pm-1am Sun;
Ⓜ Tribunal; ♿ 👶

With Asian and African decoration,
creative Mediterranean cooking
and a noisy Spanish clientele, Co-
nache is a hub of barrio life and is
as good for breakfast as for dinner.

🍴 CRÊPERIE MA BRETAGNE
Crepes   €€

☎ 91 531 77 74; Calle de San Vicente
Ferrer 9; ⏱ 8.30pm-1am Thu-Sun, to
2am Fri & Sat; Ⓜ Tribunal

What a wonderful little place this
is – dark, candlelit and all about
delicious crepes for main courses
and desserts. You'll never want
to see a crepe again after eating

here, but overindulgence in such
a cosy atmosphere is a great way
to go out.

🍴 HOME BURGER BAR
Burger Bar   €€

☎ 91 522 97 28; www.homeburger
bar.com; Calle del Espíritu Santo 12;
⏱ 1.30-4pm & 8.30pm-midnight
Tue-Sat, 2-4pm & 8.30-11pm Sun;
Ⓜ Tribunal; ♿ 👶

There are times when you just
need a burger. Home Burger Bar
is outstanding, with an interesting mix of vegetarian, gourmet
and classic hamburgers served by
friendly waiters in an American
diner-style setting. The meat is
'ecologically sound' and, in the
Spanish style, medium-rare (they'll
cook it more if you ask).

🍴 LA ISLA DEL TESORO
Vegetarian   €€

☎ 91 593 14 40; www.isladeltesoro.net,
in Spanish; Calle de Manuela Malasaña 3;
⏱ 1-4pm & 9pm-midnight; Ⓜ Bilbao;
Ⓥ

Unlike some vegetarian restaurants that seem to work on the
philosophy that basic décor signifies healthy food, La Isla del Tesoro
is loaded with quirky charm and
the food is creative and excellent.
It's started to lose some friends for
the sense that they're keen to free-
up your table for the next punters
on weekend nights, but that's our
only criticism.

LA MUSA *Fusion* €€

☎ 91 448 75 58; www.lamusa.com.es;
Calle de Manuela Malasaña 18; ⏱ 9am-
1am Mon-Thu, 9am-2am Fri, 1pm-2am Sat,
1pm-1am Sun; Ⓜ Bilbao or San Bernardo

A local favourite of Malasaña's hip
young crowd, La Musa has designer décor, lounge music on the
sound system and food that will
live long in the memory. It doesn't
take reservations so sidle up to the
bar, put your name on the waiting
list and soak up the ambient buzz
of Malasaña at its best.

NINA
Nouvelle Cuisine €€

☎ 91 591 00 46; Calle de Manuela
Malasaña 10; ⏱ 1.30-4.30pm & 8.30pm-
12.30am Mon-Thu, to 1am Fri & Sat,
11am-4.30pm & 8.30pm-12.30am Sun;
Ⓜ Bilbao

Popular with a sophisticated
local crowd, Nina has fantastic
Mediterranean food, great service
and a character-filled dining area.
Nina can be a hard place to get a
table, and booking on weekends
is essential (the two sittings are at
9.15pm and 11.15pm).

OJALÁ *Fusion & Café* €€

☎ 91 523 27 47; Calle de San Andrés 1;
⏱ 9am-12.30am Sun-Wed, 9am-1.30am
Thu, 9am-2am Fri & Sat; Ⓜ Tribunal;
♿ 🚼

From the people who brought
you La Musa, Ojalá is every bit as
funky and with a lot more space
to enjoy it. With a lime-green
colour scheme, zany lighting and
a hip, café-style ambience, it's
an extremely cool place to hang
out. The sandy floor and cushions
downstairs make for a very chilled
space.

RIBEIRA DO MIÑO
Galician & Seafood €€

☎ 91 521 98 54; Calle de la Santa
Brigida 1; ⏱ 1-4.30pm & 8pm-midnight
Tue-Sun; Ⓜ Tribunal; ♿ 🚼

This riotously popular bar and
restaurant is where Madrileños
with a love for seafood indulge
their fantasy. The *mariscada de la
casa* (€31 for two) is a platter of
seafood that is so large that even
the hungriest of visitors will leave
satisfied. Leave your name with
the waiter and be prepared to wait
for up to an hour to get a table.

🍸 DRINK

Malasaña's loyalty to the spirit of
la movida madrileña continues and
the bars here are temples to the
1980s (or just before or after but
rarely much beyond that). On the
surface it's all about retro music
and dressing down but not everyone who comes here is a nostalgic
rocker and the crowd can be pretty
diverse. Conde Duque is the place
for a more chilled atmosphere.

Let the words run free at Café Comercial

▼ BAR EL 2D *Bar*
☎ 91 445 88 39; Calle de Velarde 24;
🕒 1pm-2am Sun-Thu, 1pm-2.30am Fri &
Sat; Ⓜ Tribunal; ♿
One of the enduring symbols of *la movida madrileña*, El 2D's fluted columns, 1970s-brown walls and 1980s music suggest that it hasn't quite arrived in the 21st century yet. No-one seems to care, mind you.

▼ CAFÉ COMERCIAL *Café*
☎ 91 521 56 55; Glorieta de Bilbao 7;
🕒 8am-1am Sun-Thu, to 2am Fri & Sat;
Ⓜ Bilbao
This glorious old Madrid café proudly fights a rearguard action against progress with heavy leath-

er seats, abundant marble and old-style waiters. Once the Madrid equivalent of the literary cafés of Paris' Left Bank, Café Comercial is a true Madrid landmark that now draws a broad cross-section of Madrileños.

▼ CAFÉ PEPE BOTELLA *Bar*
☎ 91 522 43 09; Calle de San Andrés 12;
🕒 11am-2.30am; Ⓜ Bilbao or Tribunal
As good in the wee small hours as it is in the afternoon, Café Pepe Botella is a classy bar with green velvet benches, marble-topped tables and old photos and mirrors covering the walls. It's one of the most popular and enduring drinking holes in the barrio and worth a visit.

▼ CAFEINA *Café-Bar*
Calle del Pez 18; ◷ 3pm-3am Mon-Sat; Ⓜ Callao or Tribunal; ♿ ⚥
Just before Malasaña disappears into the seedy hinterland of Gran Vía, Cafeina is a lovely down-tempo bar with soft lighting, cool music and a mellow crowd. On weekends, DJs spice things up a bit upstairs.

▼ EL CAFÉ SIN NOMBRE
Café-Bar
☎ 91 548 09 72; Calle del Conde Duque 10; ◷ 3pm-3am Mon-Thu, 8pm-3.30am Fri & Sat; Ⓜ Plaza de España or Ventura Rodríguez; ⚥
The 'Café With No Name' is one of Conde Duque's many well-kept secrets, the sort of place where in-the-know Madrileños gravitate while the tourists go elsewhere. With its exposed brickwork and wooden beams, it's a classy look that comes alive late at night with the dull roar of Madrileños at play.

▼ EL JARDÍN SECRETO
Café-Bar
☎ 91 541 80 23; Calle del Conde Duque 2; ◷ 5.30pm-1.30am Sun-Thu, 6.30pm-2.30am Fri & Sat; Ⓜ Plaza de España
One of our favourite places to drink in Madrid, 'the Secret Garden' has a hip café-style ambience in a barrio that's one of Madrid's best-kept secrets. It's at its best on a summer's evening but the atmosphere never misses a beat – candlelit, cosy and intimate with a real buzz among the young professional crowd.

▼ EL PARNASILLO *Bar*
☎ 91 447 00 79; cafeparnasillo@terra.es; Calle de San Andrés 33; ◷ 2.30pm-3am Sun-Thu, to 3.30am Fri & Sat; Ⓜ Bilbao; ♿ ⚥
Another of the grand old literary cafés to have survived close to the Glorieta de Bilbao, El Parnasillo has old-world décor with muted art-nouveau murals adorning the walls, but is a favourite drinking hole for the diverse crowd drawn to Malasaña.

▼ KABOKLA *Bar*
☎ 91 532 59 66; www.kabokla.es, in Spanish; Calle de San Vicente Ferrer 55; ◷ 10pm-1am Tue-Thu, 6pm-late Fri, 2.30-6.30pm & 10.30pm-late Sat, 2.30-10pm Sun; Ⓜ Noviciado
Run by Brazilians and dedicated to all things Brazilian, Kabokla is terrific. Live Brazilian groups play some nights from around 10pm. Otherwise, the DJ gets the crowd dancing, fuelled by Madrid's smoothest caipirinhas.

▼ LA PALMERA *Bar*
Calle de la Palma 67; ◷ 7.30pm-2am Mon-Sat; Ⓜ Tribunal
Tucked away in the narrow lanes of Conde Duque, this tiny place is covered in blue and yellow tiles

Rendezvous with Madrileños at El Jardín Secreto (p123)

and draws an artsy crowd that comes to sit a while at the small wooden tables and nurse a drink or two. The atmosphere is very low-key.

▼ LA VACA AUSTERA *Bar*
☎ 91 523 14 87; Calle de la Palma 20;
🕒 9pm-3am Mon-Sat; Ⓜ Tribunal
Old habits die hard at this veteran bar that once played host to some of the best bands of *la movida* in the 1980s. Its warehouse feel won't be to everyone's taste, but it's a local icon and a totally

unpretentious place to hear alternative rock music.

▼ LA VÍA LÁCTEA
Bar & Nightclub
☎ 91 446 75 81; Calle de Velarde 18;
🕒 7.30pm-3am; Ⓜ Tribunal
This living, breathing and somewhat grungy relic of *la movida* remains a Malasaña favourite for a mixed, informal crowd that seems to live for the 1980s. Expect long queues to get in on weekends; by early on Sunday morning, anything goes.

▼ MUSHOTOKU CAFE
Lounge Bar

Calle de Santa Bárbara 8; ⏱ 6pm-midnight Tue & Wed, 7.30pm-2am Thu-Sat; ♿ ; Ⓜ Metro Tribunal

Tiny, black-walled and laid-back funky, Mushotoku is a mellow place to nurse your drink. On Friday and Saturday a DJ spins minimalist techno tunes and although there's no real space to dance, this place is all about dancing on the inside.

⭐ PLAY

Most of Malasaña's bars have dance floors and so you could easily nurse a drink or two and then get up to shake your thing without leaving the bar. As bars start to close, the barrio's streets fill with people who aren't yet ready to head home. Just follow the crowd.

⭐ LIVE MUSIC

⭐ CAFÉ LA PALMA *Live Music*

☎ 91 522 50 31; www.cafelapalma.com, in Spanish; Calle de la Palma 62; admission free-€6; ⏱ 4pm-2am Sun-Thu, 4pm-3.30am Fri & Sat; Ⓜ San Bernardo

It's amazing how much variety Café La Palma has packed into its labyrinth of rooms. Live shows featuring hot local bands are held at the back, while DJs mix up the front. Some rooms have a café style, while others look like an Arab tea room, pillows on the floor and all. Every night is a little different, so expect to be surprised.

⭐ NIGHTCLUBS

⭐ LAYDOWN REST CLUB
Nightclub

☎ 91 548 79 37; www.laydown.es, in Spanish; Plaza Mostenses 9; ⏱ 9.30pm-2am Wed & Thu, 9.30pm-3am Fri & Sat, 12.30-6pm & 9.30pm-2am Sun; Ⓜ Plaza de España or Noviciado

Laydown Rest Club is whiter-than-white and completely devoid of tables – you recline with your drink (it's also a restaurant) Roman-style on beds, served by toga-clad waiters with huge feather fans. The DJs ensure that there's no danger of falling asleep.

>CHAMBERÍ & ARGÜELLES

Chamberí and Argüelles, north of the city centre, are among Madrid's most traditional barrios (neighbourhoods) and have become the heart-land of Madrid's newly rich. If you could live anywhere in Madrid, chances are that you'd choose here (house prices are soaring) amid the leafy streets and away from the tourists. Great restaurants are dotted around the barrios, shopping is outstanding, particularly along Calle de Fuencar-ral, and although there are few sights worth seeing, both Chamberí and Argüelles have a real neighbourhood feel.

For the purposes of this book, Chamberí stretches westward from Paseo de la Castellana in the east, and runs into Argüelles in the west. Argüelles in turn doglegs south, spreading west from Calle de la Princesa. Sloping parkland along Paseo del Pintor Rosales closes off the area to the west. There aren't many tourist sights in the area, but the atmosphere is delightful and visiting these barrios is all about living like a Madrileño in one of Europe's most agreeable cities.

CHAMBERÍ & ARGÜELLES

◎ SEE
Museo de América 1 A2
Museo Sorolla 2 G3
Parque del Oeste 3 A2
Teleférico 4 A5
Templo de Debod 5 B6

⌂ SHOP
Antigüedades Hom ...(see 12)
Calzados Cantero 6 E3
Diedro 7 E4
Los Bebés de
Chamberí 8 E3

▥ EAT
Casa Ricardo 9 D3
Collage 10 E4
El Brillante 11 E3
El Pedrusco 12 E3
Il Casone 13 E3
Las Tortillas de
Gabino 14 G3
Restaurante La
Giralda 15 E4
Sagaretxe 16 E3
Santceloni 17 G2
Sergi Arola Gastro 18 G4

▼ DRINK
Locandita 19 E3

★ PLAY
Clamores 20 E4
Honky Tonk 21 F4
Moma 56 ....22 G2
Zensei 23 C2

Please see over for map

👁 SEE

👁 MUSEO DE AMÉRICA
☎ 91 549 26 41; http://museodeamerica.mcu.es, in Spanish; Avenida de los Reyes Católicos 6; adult/student/senior & child under 18yr €3/1.50/free, free Sun; ⏱ 9.30am-3pm Tue-Sat, 10am-3pm Sun & holidays; Ⓜ Moncloa

Dedicated to Spain's former colonies in the Americas, this museum provides a fascinating insight into Imperial Spain.

👁 MUSEO SOROLLA
☎ 91 310 15 84; http://museosorolla.mcu.es, in Spanish; Paseo del General Martínez Campos 37; adult/under 18yr, student & senior €3/free, free Sun; ⏱ 9.30am-8pm Tue-Sat, 10am-3pm Sun & holidays; Ⓜ Iglesia

The Valencian artist Joaquín Sorolla immortalised the clear Mediterranean light of the Valencian coast and his former Madrid house – a quiet mansion surrounded by lush gardens and with a delightful Andalucian patio – with this gallery, containing the fullest collection of his works.

👁 PARQUE DEL OESTE
Avenida del Arco de la Victoria; Ⓜ Moncloa

Sloping down the hill behind the Moncloa Metro station, Parque del Oeste (West Park) is quite beautiful, with plenty of shady corners to recline under a tree in the heat of the day and fine views out to the west towards Casa de Campo.

👁 TELEFÉRICO
☎ 91 541 11 18; www.teleferico.com, in Spanish; Paseo del Pintor Rosales; adult 1-way/return €3.50/5.10, child 3-7yr 1-way/return €3.40/4; ⏱ hours vary; Ⓜ Argüelles

One of the world's most horizontal cable cars (never more than 40m above the ground) putters out from the slopes of La Rosaleda, a delightful stand of green perched on the ridge looking out over western Madrid. The *teleférico* (cable car) travels for 2.5km across into the depths of Casa de Campo, Madrid's enormous green open space to the west of the city centre.

AREAS OF INTEREST
To get a taste of Chamberí, one of Madrid's most agreeable barrios, head for **Plaza de Olavide**, a green square with children's playgrounds and a fountain. When the weather's warm, park yourself at one of the outdoor tables (competition is fierce!) of the bars that surround the plaza. On Sunday mornings, **Calle de Fuencarral** is closed to traffic from 10am to 2pm between Glorieta de Bilbao and Glorieta de Quevedo. That's when all the barrio comes out to play.

See Malasaña & Conde Duque Map pp116–17

See Los Austrias, Sol & Centro Map pp42–3

◉ TEMPLO DE DEBOD
☎ 91 366 74 15; www.munimadrid.es
/templodebod/; Calle de Ferraz 1;
admission free; 🕑 10am-2pm & 6-8pm
Tue-Fri, 10am-2pm Sat & Sun Apr-Sep,
9.45am-1.45pm & 4.15-6.15pm Tue-Fri,
10am-2pm Sat & Sun Oct-Mar; Ⓜ Ventura Rodríguez

This Egyptian temple was saved
from the rising waters of Lake
Nasser in southern Egypt when
Egyptian president Gamal Abdel
Nasser built the Aswan High Dam.
After 1968 it was sent block by
block to Spain as a gesture of
thanks to Spanish archaeologists.

Templo de Debod: Egypt in Madrid

🛍 SHOP
Most of the major brand-names
have shops in this barrio, but there
is a handful of smaller boutiques
with plenty of character.

🛍 ANTIGÜEDADES HOM
Antiques & Crafts
☎ 91 594 20 17; Calle de Juan de Austria
31; 🕑 5-8pm Mon-Wed, noon-2pm &
5-8pm Thu & Fri; Ⓜ Iglesia

Specialising in antique Spanish
fans, this tiny shop is a wonderful
place to browse for a special gift,
especially delicately painted fans
and fans made with bone. It's only
open most afternoons because
the owner spends the morning
restoring the fans you see for sale.

🛍 CALZADOS CANTERO *Shoes*
☎ 91 447 07 35; Plaza de Olavide 12;
🕑 10am-2pm & 4.45-8.30pm Mon-Sat;
Ⓜ Quevedo, Iglesia or Bilbao

A charming old-world shoe store,
Calzados Cantero sells a range of
of shoes at rock-bottom prices. But
it's most famous for its rope-soled
alpargatas (espadrilles), which
start from €5.50.

🛍 DIEDRO *Gifts & Fashion*
☎ 91 444 59 59; www.diedro.com; Calle
de Sagasta 17; 🕑 10am-10pm Mon-Sat,
noon-10pm Sun; Ⓜ Bilbao

One of the most innovative gift
shops in Madrid, Diedro has designer jewellery, clothes, stationery

and homewares. It's a wonderful space spanning just about every taste, as long as it's stylish.

🛍 LOS BEBÉS DE CHAMBERÍ
Children's Fashion
☎ 91 535 13 25; www.losbebesdechamberi.com, in Spanish; Calle de Gonzalo de Córdoba 7; 🕙 11am-2.30pm & 5.30-8.30pm Tue-Sat, 5-8.30pm Mon; Ⓜ Quevedo

This small shop showcases that wonderful individuality of Spanish children's clothes; you'll leave laden with bags for your own kids and for friends back home.

🍴 EAT

You need to know where to look to find the best restaurants in these barrios as they're reasonably spread out, but they're always worth finding.

🍴 CASA RICARDO
Spanish €€
☎ 91 447 61 19; www.casaricardo.net, in Spanish; Calle de Fernando El Católico 31; 🕙 1.15-4pm & 9pm-midnight Mon-Sat, 1.15-4pm Sun; Ⓜ Argüelles or Quevedo

This brilliant little 1930s-era *taberna* (tavern) is tucked away in residential Argüelles. Its speciality is *callos* (tripe) but there's plenty more. Like any old Spanish bar worth its salt, it's cramped, adorned with bullfighting photos and is aimed at aficionados rather than tourists.

🍴 COLLAGE
Scandinavian €€
☎ 91 448 45 62; www.restaurante collage.com, in Spanish; Calle de Olíd 6; 🕙 1-4pm Mon, 1-4pm & 9pm-midnight Tue-Sat; Ⓜ Quevedo or Bilbao

One of our favourite restaurants in Trafalgar, Collage serves wonderful food (the *rollitos de alce*, 'reindeer rolls', are a spectacular entrée) and the whole atmosphere is casual but sleek in a Swedish kind of way.

🍴 EL BRILLANTE
Snacks & Tapas €
☎ 91 448 19 88; Calle de Eloy Gonzalo 14; 🕙 6.30am-12.30am; Ⓜ Quevedo

Famous for its *chocolate con churros* or *porras* (deep-fried doughnut strips), *bocadillos* (sandwiches; the *bocadillo de calamares* is an old favourite) and breezy atmosphere, El Brillante is a barrio classic.

🍴 EL PEDRUSCO *Spanish* €€
☎ 91 446 88 33; www.elpedrusco dealdealcorvo.com, in Spanish; Calle de Juan de Austria 27; 🕙 1.30-4pm Mon-Thu, 1.30-4pm & 9pm-midnight Fri & Sat; Ⓜ Iglesia

The roasted meats at this fine restaurant are as good as any in this city. The *menú segoviano* (€23) includes succulent roast lamb, while the *menú pedrusco* (€25) has some vegetable respite, at least until the steak arrives.

🍴 IL CASONE *Italian* €€
☎ 91 591 62 66; Calle de Trafalgar 25; ☾ 1.30-4pm & 8.30-11.30pm; Ⓜ Quevedo or Iglesia

With its outdoor tables on the lovely Plaza de Olavide, reasonable prices and fresh and inventive Italian cooking, Il Casone is most excellent.

🍴 LAS TORTILLAS DE GABINO
Spanish €€€
☎ 91 319 75 05; www.lastortillasdegabino.com, in Spanish; Calle de Rafael Calvo 20; ☾ 1.30-4pm & 9-11.30pm Mon-Fri, 9-11.30pm Sat; Ⓜ Iglesia

It's a brave Spanish chef that fiddles with the iconic *tortilla de patatas (Spanish omelette),* but the results here are delicious – tortilla with cockles, with octopus, with all manner of surprising combinations.

WORTH THE TRIP
The Michelin-starred **Santceloni** (☎ 91 210 88 40; www.restaurantesantceloni.com; Paseo de la Castellana 57; meals €130; ☾ 2-4pm & 9-11pm Mon-Fri, 9-11pm Sat; Ⓜ Gregorio Marañón) is one of Madrid's best restaurants, with luxury Asian-inspired décor and food that wins plaudits from discerning food-lovers from across Spain and abroad. Each dish is exquisite. Santceloni is just north of the Metro exit on the west side of Paseo de la Castellana. The doorway is next to the entrance of the Hesperia Hotel.

🍴 RESTAURANTE LA GIRALDA
Andalucian & Tapas €€
☎ 91 445 17 43; www.restauranteslagiralda.com, in Spanish; Calle de Hartzembusch 12 & 15; ☾ 1-4pm & 8pm-midnight Mon & Wed-Sat, 1-4pm Tue, closed Aug; Ⓜ Bilbao

For nearly every kind of fried or fresh Mediterranean seafood you can imagine (and many you can't), Restaurante La Giralda feels like being in Sevilla. The quality is high so it's hugely popular but the downstairs area is surprisingly large.

🍴 SAGARETXE
Basque & Tapas €€
☎ 91 446 25 88; www.sagaretxe.com; Calle de Eloy Gonzalo 26; ☾ noon-5pm & 7pm-midnight Sun-Wed, noon-5pm & 7pm-12.30am Thu, noon-5pm & 7pm-1am Fri & Sat; Ⓜ Iglesia

One of the best Basque *pintxos* (tapas) bars in Madrid, Sagaretxe takes the stress out of taking tapas. Simply point and they'll put any of the wonderful selection on a plate for you. Better still, order the *surtido de 8/12 pintxos* (your own selection of 8/12 tapas) for €14/20.

🍴 SERGI AROLA GASTRO
Nouvelle Cuisine €€€
☎ 91 310 21 69; www.sergiarola.es; Calle de Zurbano 31; ☾ 2-3.30pm & 9-11.30pm Mon-Fri, 9-11.30pm Sat; Ⓜ Alonso Martínez

Sergi Arola, a Catalan acolyte of Ferran Adriá, has opened his personalised temple to all that's innovative in Spanish gastronomy. You pay for the privilege of eating here (the standard Menú Gastro costs €130) and servings are small-ish. But oh, what tastes…

🍸 DRINK

Small bars loaded with local character are a barrio speciality.

🍸 LOCANDITA *Café-Bar*
☎ 91 444 11 97; Calle de Fuencarral 148; 🕓 7am-10.30pm Mon-Thu, 9am-10.30pm Fri-Sun; Ⓜ Quevedo
Good for a drink or pastry at any hour of the day, this friendly little bar is a bright place to rest during your Chamberí explorations.

⭐ PLAY

⭐ CLAMORES
Live Music
☎ 91 445 79 38; www.salaclamores.com; Calle de Alburquerque 14; admission €7-25; 🕓 6pm-3am Sun-Thu, 6pm-4am Fri & Sat; Ⓜ Bilbao
A classic jazz café that doesn't mind mixing pop, flamenco, Brazilian or other world music, so the fusion sounds here always make for an interesting night. Live shows begin as early as 9pm but sometimes really get going after 1am on weekends.

⭐ HONKY TONK *Live Music*
☎ 91 445 61 91; www.clubhonky.com, in Spanish; Calle de Covarrubias 24; 🕓 9pm-5am Mon-Thu, 9pm-5.30am Fri & Sat, 10pm-5am Sun; Ⓜ Alonso Martínez
Despite the name, this is a great place to see live rock 'n' roll, though many acts have a little country or some blues thrown in too. It's a fun vibe in a smallish club, so arrive early as it fills up fast.

⭐ MOMA 56 *Nightclub*
☎ 91 399 09 00; www.moma56.com; Calle de José Abascal 56; admission €15; 🕓 11.30pm-6am Wed-Sat; Ⓜ Gregorio Marañón
Two words: beautiful people. Get your Prada gear on and that studied look of sophistication and join the small-time celebrities and owners of the flashy sports cars parked out front. The décor (think red padded walls, red lighting) is as sleek as the too-cool crowd who shake off their pretensions once the live percussion fuses into DJ House.

⭐ ZENSEI *Spa*
☎ 91 549 60 49; www.zensei.net; Calle de Blasco de Garay 64; 🕓 10am-10pm Mon-Sat; Ⓜ Moncloa or Quevedo
This Japanese relaxation centre promises the ultimate in Zen massage, acupuncture, reiki, shiatsu and yoga, not to mention origami and Japanese tea-ceremony classes. You'll come out floating on air.

>SNAPSHOTS

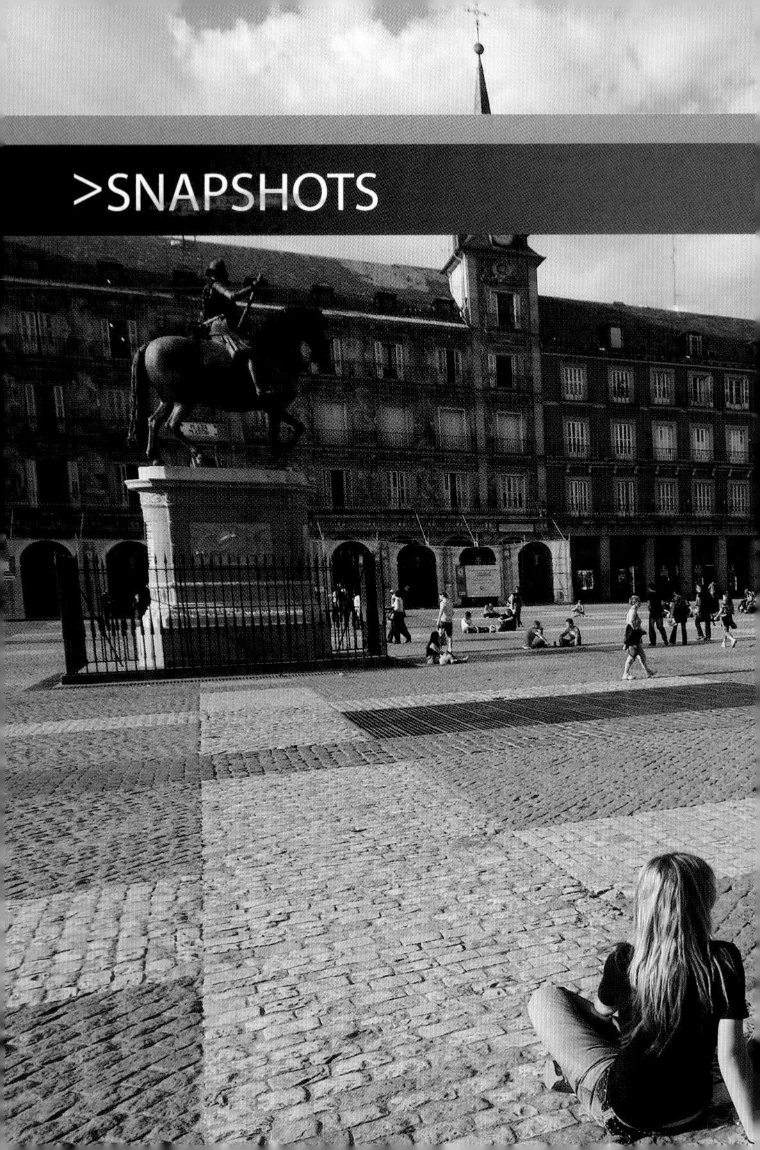

Madrid is a city where local knowledge is everything. There are barrios where certain activities are over-represented (eg live music in Huertas, shopping in Salamanca), but mostly they're spread across the city, which means planning well before you set out. This chapter highlights the best in each category to help you tailor your own unique trip.

Chill out and watch the world go by at Madrid's iconic Plaza Mayor (p10)

ACCOMMODATION

Madrid's accommodation is top-notch and the price-to-quality ratio is exceptionally high. Madrid is also so compact and so well served by its excellent Metro system that just about any hotel or *hostal* (one- to three-star hostel) that you choose will be a near-perfect base for exploring the city.

The most welcome innovation on the accommodation scene has been the sudden proliferation of boutique hotels that combine chic minimalism, supreme levels of comfort and facilities. The best of these marry sleek-lined interiors with structures of considerable old-world architectural elegance. Although you'll pay a fistful of euros for some of them, there are some which let you sleep in the heart of Madrid for as little as €100 – rare in a major European city.

Madrid's cheaper accommodation choices have not been left behind in this rush to embrace the style-conscious. *Hostales* that look like a Spanish grandmother's drawing room are slowly being overtaken by those which have tidied up their act with new furniture, a lick of paint and splashes of character without losing the charm of their family-run ambience. Unusually, you'll often find private bathrooms and TVs in most rooms. Those with dorm-type digs have even come to understand that style is important and most have transformed into multipurpose spaces offering a range of activities, traveller advice and places to kick back with others.

For those who love to have a room with a balcony, or at least a view, Madrid presents a difficult choice. On the one hand, having a front-row seat to the street theatre of central Madrid means that you won't mind passing your down-time in your room because you'll feel in the midst of it without leaving your room. At the same time, Madrid is an extremely noisy city. If you're here from Thursday to Sunday, especially in summer, the dull roar of crowds may not abate until close to sunrise. If you're a light sleeper and don't plan on joining Madrid's nightly outdoor celebration, you *will* find it difficult to sleep. That means choosing between an *interior* (a room on the inside of the building looking onto a patio or, more often, a small light well) or an *exterior* (with windows or balconies onto the street). The noise problem is particularly acute in Huertas, Malasaña, Chueca and just about anywhere in central Madrid, less so in Salamanca or Chamberí.

High season is most of the year for most hotels and many don't alter their rates significantly during the year. In slow times, such as the depths of winter (late November to December, except Christmas, and mid-January to March), hoteliers may do deals, depending on whether trade fairs are being held. Many of the top, business-oriented hotels also cut good deals for weekend stays. Websites offering reservations for Madrid hotels and *hostales* abound. Some of the better ones include www.apartmentsapart .com/madrid_hotels with last-minute deals, and www.madrid-on-line.com for self-service booking. Try www.30madrid.com for €30 deals.

BEST BOUTIQUE HOTELS
> Petit Palace Posada del Peine (www .hthoteles.com)
> Alicia Room Mate (www.room-mate hoteles.com)
> Hotel Meninas (www.hotelmeninas.com)
> Hotel Abalú (www.hotelabalu.com)
> Quo (www.hotelesquo.com)
> Hotel de las Letras (www.hoteldelas letras.com)

BEST INTIMATE STAY
> Hotel Miau (www.hotelmiau.com)
> Hostel Plaza Mayor (www.h-plaza mayor.com)
> Chic & Basic Colors (www.chicandbasic .com)
> Hostal La Zona (www.lazona.com)

BEST LAP OF LUXURY
> Hotel Puerta de América (www .hotelpuertamerica.com)
> Ritz (www.ritzmadrid.com)
> Hotel Urban (www.derbyhotels.com)
> AC Santo Mauro (www.ac-hotels .com)
> Westin Palace (www.westinpalace madrid.com)

BEST BACKPACKER SCENE
> Cat's Hostel (www.catshostel.com)
> Mad Hostel (www.madhostel.com)
> Los Amigos Backpacker's Hostel (www .losamigoshostel.com)
> Albergue Juvenil (www.ajmadrid.es)
> La Posada de Huertas (www.laposad adehuertas.com)

BARS & CLUBS

Madrid has more bars than any city in the world – six, in fact, for every 100 inhabitants. In Madrid a bar is a meeting place, a social hub of barrio life for all ages and a place to eat tapas as much as to drink alcohol. As such, it's one that the teetotallers among us can enjoy as much as those of us who like our beer, wine or something stronger. Yes, they drink here more often than elsewhere, but it's extremely rare to see a drunk Madrileño. Going to a bar is about meeting friends and enjoying life, and alcohol is an accompaniment to these noble pursuits, rarely the primary purpose.

The majority of Madrid's bars are local watering holes that draw a mainly local clientele. Some of these have wonderful tiled façades, while others are basic, or what's known in Spanish as *cutre* (which translates roughly as 'rough-and-ready') – walk past these at your peril, for these are often where you'll find the best tapas and the most authentic atmosphere. Until recently, these were the only types of bars that Madrid had to offer.

In the last five to 10 years, however, a sudden proliferation of funky new bars has swept through the city. The designer interiors suggest Barcelona and the lounge or chill-out music evokes Ibiza, but the ambience is unmistakably Madrid.

As for bars, so too for clubs, although the distinction between the two is often blurred in the after-midnight hours. Madrid's famous superclubs are still going strong, but added to these are smaller, more intimate clubs where the vibe is sophisticated in a New York kind of way. It's in the clubs that you'll most agree with Ernest Hemingway that 'Nobody goes to bed in Madrid until they have killed the night.'

Every barrio has plenty of bars, but Huertas, Chueca and Malasaña are Madrid's hedonism central; the former attracts a local and international crowd just about any night of the week, Chueca is extravagantly gay but everyone's welcome, while Malasaña is the spiritual home of *la movida madrileña*. Lavapiés and La Latina are gritty and groovy and cool all at once. Most of the bigger clubs are in the centre.

BEST BARS FOR CHILLING-OUT
> Café Belén (p108)
> El Jardín Secreto (p123)
> Areia (p108)
> Jazz Bar (p78)
> Dos Gardenias (p77)
> The Penthouse (p79)

BEST BIG CLUBS
> Cool (p56)
> Teatro Joy Eslava (p57)
> Kapital (p87)
> Room Club (p81)
> Palacio Gaviria (p57)

BEST OLD TABERNAS
> Casa Alberto (p75)
> La Venencia (p78)
> Bodega de La Ardosa (p118)
> Taberna de Antonio Sánchez (p66)
> Taberna Alhambra (p79)
> Almendro 13 (p64)
> Viva Madrid (p79)

BEST COOL CLUBS
> Costello Café & Nightclub (p56)
> Laydown Rest Club (p125)
> Museo Chicote (p112)
> Vervet (p113)
> Local Café Bar Lounge (p113)

Opposite Clubbers at Palacio Gaviria (p57) **Above** One of many bars in Malasaña

FASHION

In the 18th-century, Madrileños rioted when told by the king that they could no longer wear the sweeping capes that so distinguished them. Those days may be long gone, but they still take their fashion seriously in Madrid.

The current buzz surrounding Spanish fashion began way back in the 1980s when Spain in general and Madrid in particular embraced all that was new and experimental after the fascist austerity of the Franco years. What has changed recently is that Madrid has come to surpass Barcelona as Spain's fashion capital, and while Madrid may not yet rival Milan or Paris in Europe, Madrid's Pasarela Cibeles (p27) runway fashion shows have become increasingly important.

Colour is the key to Spanish individuality. The psychedelic colours of *la movida madrileña* in the 1980s have never really gone away and the candy-bright colours of Agatha Ruiz de la Prada (Andy Warhol was a fan of this icon of modern Madrid) have now acquired something of a middle-class respectability. This stylish-but-anything-goes approach has morphed into a fashion scene dominated by bold colours equally well-suited to the casual as to a more tailored look.

Classic and more conservative lines are the preserve of Loewe, Sybilla, Ángel Schlesser and the Madrileña Alma Aguilar. A more formal/casual mix is favoured by designers such as Amaya Arzuaga, Purificación García, Roberto Torretta and Roberto Verino. Apart from the names already mentioned, others to watch out for on the catwalk include the Madrileño Javier Larraínzar (one of the city's top *haute couture* icons), Pedro del

Hierro, Kina Fernández, Nacho Ruiz and Montesinos Alama. More clean-lined and casual is Armand Basi, while the clothes of David Delfín span the divide between edgy and exclusive.

Spain is also famous for the quality of its shoes and the designers once known only to Spaniards and Madrileñas are fast becoming fixtures on the international scene. Manolo Blahnik is perhaps the best known, and his shoes have become more a fixture at the Oscars than Penélope Cruz. Many designers also do great lines in handbags and other accessories (they wouldn't maintain the loyalty of Madrileñas if they didn't) and there's no finer exponent of the art than the hand-painted, sophisticated but fun masterpieces of Iñaki Sampedro.

The shopping explosion that began in the 1990s in Madrid shows no sign of abating and even in these troubled economic times, it looks likely to continue for years to come. With such a strong local base from which to work, Spanish designs are increasingly taking the world by storm. Although designer wear has come to dominate the Madrileño wardrobe and is capturing international headlines on the catwalk, a host of more af-fordable high-street wear is also leading the way. Just about every Madrid barrio has at least one outlet for names such as Zara (with more than 1500 shops in 73 countries), Adolfo Domínguez and Mango, which have in turn become some of Spain's leading exports. And where would we be without the cool and casual shoes of Camper? If these have been your introduction to the world of Spanish fashion, you'll very much enjoy Madrid, but don't forget that these are merely the start to a far more sophisticated look.

One of the success stories of Spanish cultural life, the Spanish fashion industry now employs more than 500,000 people (more than three times than employed by Spanish bullfighting). This is an industry which is aiming high and industry insiders admit that Spain's *fashionistas* won't be satisfied until Madrid has been elevated to the top tier of European fashion capitals. On current trends, they may not have long to wait.

BEST ICONS OF SPANISH FASHION

> Agatha Ruiz de la Prada (p92)
> Manolo Blahnik (p94)
> Purificación García (p95)

BEST FOR CATWALK CASUAL

> Amaya Arzuaga (p91)
> Armand Basi (p93)
> Davidelfín (p93)
> Adolfo Domínguez (p115)

SHOPPING

Although many cities make this claim, Madrid is definitely a shopper's paradise, even to the extent of being almost without parallel in Europe. What allows it to assert this is the mix of possibilities on offer with price tags that haven't been seen in London or Paris for decades. It's also not only about price, because Madrileños are such serious shoppers that places that don't cut it in terms of quality simply don't survive long here.

If it's clothes you're after, you'll find everything from designer boutiques and the great names of international fashion to down-and-dirty street wear that's ideal for a casual night out in Madrid. When it comes to souvenirs, yes, you *can* find plenty of places to get your name printed on a bullfighting or flamenco poster if you're that way inclined, but why not instead take home an exquisite *abanico* (Spanish fan), hand-painted ceramic tile or a papier-mâché figure that you'd only find in Madrid?

The most important thing to remember is that shopping in the Spanish capital is all about finding your barrio style because there's one that's sure to suit your lifestyle (or the lifestyle you'd like to lead).

The upmarket barrio of Salamanca is designer central, the sort of place that shoppers parade through, dressed in the latest fashions and in search of tomorrow's style so that their next promenade is even more stylish. This barrio lives and breathes boutiques that represent the best in Spanish fashion, from the larger chains to the smaller, alternative stores, from *prêt-a-porter* to consciously casual lines. Calle de Serrano (p19) is the most important thoroughfare in this regard, but the boutiques fan out across the barrio, lining streets such as Calle de Claudio Coello, Calle de Jorge Juan or Calle de José Ortega y Gasset.

Chueca seems to have a rule that no shops above a certain size will be allowed. Its small shops are often a match for Salamanca, but with more quirky touches that appeal to the barrio's large gay population, and friendlier, more laid-back service. As such, Chueca acts as something akin to a shopping bridge between the glamour of Salamanca and Malasaña, where it's all about comfort and dressing down and finding something outlandish or offbeat, always with an eye on the latest street fashions; in Malasaña it's about a studied underground look or an alternative club aesthetic. As such, Malasaña is the barrio to set off to in search of clothing where all things retro are recurring themes, as is just about anything else that wouldn't be seen in Salamanca.

If it's designer jewellery or other accessories with that Spanish flair for colour that you dreamt of as a reminder of your visit to Madrid, you could check out the eastern end of Chueca. Then again, you're just as likely to find it in La Latina, especially close to Calle de la Cava Baja.

We've left downtown Madrid (Los Austrias, Sol y Centro) until last because it may have the largest number of shops anywhere in Madrid, but it's something of a catch-all with no discernible personality of its own. It's here that you'll find the big names of high-street fashion. OK, these aren't the most creative choices, but they remain staples of the Madrileño shopping diet and they're an excellent last resort if you don't find what you're looking for elsewhere. If central Madrid does have a forte, it's that this is where you'll find the best (and worst!) souvenirs in Madrid.

The peak shopping season is during *las rebajas,* the annual winter and summer sales when prices are slashed on just about everything.

BEST SHOPPING STREETS

> Calle de Serrano, Salamanca (pictured opposite; p19) – Spanish designer fashions
> Calle de José Ortega y Gasset, Salamanca (p95) – International designer fashions
> Calle de Piamonte, Chueca – Designer accessories
> Calle de Fuencarral, Malasaña – Casual street wear
> Calle de Agusto Figueroa, Chueca – Shoes

BEST FOR QUALITY SOUVENIRS

> El Arco Artesanía (p46)
> Antigua Casa Talavera (p45)
> Fortunata – La Tienda de Madrid (p48)
> Casa de Diego (p46)
> Gil (p73)

ARCHITECTURE

Madrid's architecture bears beautiful traces of numerous historical styles (see p160), and a host of world-class contemporary architects are also increasingly leaving their mark upon the city.

Richard Rogers' new Terminal Four (T4) for Madrid's Barajas Airport opened in 2006 and is a stunning, curvaceous work of art. The other major urban renewal project is the transformation of the M-30 beltway along the Río Manzanares in the southwest into 50 hectares of land-scaped greenery.

The Madrid-based Rafael Moneo, whose most famous international works include the bizarre, bulging cathedral of Los Angeles (2000), was responsible for the marvellous restoration of the Antigua Estación de Atocha. This latter work is credited with halting the tendency of Madrid's builders to tear down the old in favour of characterless new structures. His latest project was the stunningly successful modernisation and extension of the iconic Museo del Prado.

Another transformational project in recent years is the extension of the Centro de Arte Reina Sofía by French architect Jean Nouvel, while Henry Cobb, Sir Norman Foster and César Pelli have begun to shape the cityscape at the northern end of the Paseo de la Castellana with designer skyscrapers.

BEST OF THE OLD
> Real Casa de la Panaderia (p10)
> Palacio de Comunicaciones (p85)
> Edificio Metrópolis (p41)
> Sociedad General de Autores y Editores (p104)
> Palacio Real (p14)
> Plaza de Toros Monumental de las Ventas (p90)

BEST OF THE NEW
> Centro de Arte Reina Sofía (p16)
> Terminal Four, Barajas Airport (p162)
> Hotel Puerta de América (p137)
> Antigua Estación de Atocha (p72)
> Caixa Forum (p84)

ART

The Spanish capital is one of the most important art cities anywhere in the world. Art has been deeply woven into the fabric of Madrid society since the country's golden age in the 17th century. As with most major cultural forms, any Spanish artists keen to make their name on the national or international stage have ended up in Madrid, and masters such as Goya, Velázquez, Picasso and Dalí all took Madrid by storm and left their mark. Put simply, almost everything that is good about Spanish art is on display in Madrid.

A thriving local creative scene has always drawn the attention of Europe's art-conscious world and even master painters with no other connection to Madrid – Rubens, Van Dyck, Botticelli and Tintoretto – appear in the city, lending a breadth and depth of artistic styles that few cities in the world can match.

Madrid's artistic hub is along the Paseo del Prado, which is home to three world-class galleries – the Prado, Reina Sofía and Thyssen, as they are known to Madrileños. Big-name temporary exhibitions – Picasso, Tintoretto and Sisley are among those to have appeared in Madrid in recent years – are regular events and perfectly complement and even serve to amplify what are already astonishing permanent exhibitions.

But restricting yourself to the big three along Madrid's Golden Mile of Art would be a shame, for the art-lover in you will discover a host of smaller but nonetheless rich galleries elsewhere in the city.

BEST MAJOR ART GALLERIES
> Museo del Prado (p12)
> Centro de Arte Reina Sofía (p16)
> Museo Thyssen-Bornemisza (p84)
> Real Academia de Bellas Artes de San Fernando (p44)

BEST OF THE REST
> Museo Lázaro Galdiano (p90)
> Museo Sorolla (p127)
> Museo Municipal de Arte Contemporáneo (p115)
> Museo de la Escultura Abstracta (p90)
> Galería Moriarty (p104)

BULLFIGHTING

An epic drama of blood and sand or a cruel blood 'sport' which has no place in modern Europe? This most enduring and controversial of Spanish traditions is all this and more, and has been immortalised in literature (think Ernest Hemingway's *The Sun Also Rises* or *Death in the Afternoon*) and art, with Picasso's cubist forms perfectly capturing this grotesque yet strangely elegant art form. Perhaps it was best summed up by Hemingway, who described it as 'a wonderful nightmare'.

Whatever your opinion, an afternoon at *la corrida* (bullfighting) is an essential part of Madrid life, particularly during the month-long season

at the Plaza de Toros Monumental de las Ventas (pictured left; p90) that begins with the Fiesta de San Isidro on 15 May. This is the world's premier bullfighting season at Spain's most prestigious venue – when *toreros* (bullfighters) put in a starring performance at Las Ventas, their career is made.

On an afternoon ticket there are generally six bulls and three star *toreros* dressed in the dazzling *traje de luces* (suit of lights), as well as their *cuadrilla* (teams). Despite the serious business of death that pervades *la corrida,* a day out at the bullring is a festive occasion with a brass band playing *pasa dobles* (double-step), A-list celebrities and aficionados dressed to the nines, and wine flowing freely.

To understand a little about how Spaniards view bullfighting, remember that listings of upcoming *corridas* and reports from the ring are covered in the culture (not sport) section of major newspapers.

FOOTBALL

When it comes to history, Real Madrid's record in major competitions is unrivalled, and you should on no account miss a visit to the Estadio Santiago Bernabéu (pictured below; p20). If you're a football fan, such a visit can easily take on the quality of a pilgrimage, and attending a match (the season runs from September to May) is the ultimate.

In the late 1990s and early 2000s, Real Madrid became a byword for sporting glamour and celebrity. Under the stewardship of the club president, construction magnate Florentino Perez, the world's most expensively assembled team to date won numerous trophies and earned the title of 'los galácticos'. It all fell apart in the three years following 2003 (the longest period in the club's history without a trophy); Perez resigned in 2006. Although Real Madrid finally won La Liga again in 2007 and 2008, it was not until 2009, after another trophy-less season, that things began to change. Perez returned as club president and began to purchase 'los galácticos' Mark II, smashing Real Madrid's own world record transfer fee first with Kaká (£56 million), then Cristiano Ronaldo (£80). Whether it translates into a new golden era remains to be seen.

It comes as a surprise to many visitors to Madrid, however, that a significant proportion of the population can't stand Real Madrid and actually support the capital's other team, Atlético Madrid, the third most successful team in Spanish history. Atlético, which has something of a cult following, attracts passionate support, with supporters of the *rojiblancos* (red-and-whites) declaring theirs to be the real Madrid team, unlike the reviled and aristocratic Madridistas up the road.

GAY & LESBIAN MADRID

Madrid is one of the most gay-friendly cities in the world and its tolerance and anything-goes nightlife make it a leading destination for gay travellers. Now is an especially good time to be gay in Madrid. Under laws passed by the Spanish Congress in June 2005, same-sex marriages now enjoy the same legal protection under Spanish law as heterosexual ones, extending into the realm of full adoption and inheritance rights. There was a conservative backlash to the law, particularly from Spain's once-powerful Catholic clergy. Opinion polls showed, however, that the reforms were supported by more than two-thirds of Spaniards.

Chueca is very much the heart and soul of gay life in Madrid and Spain and is one of Madrid's coolest, most vibrant barrios. Restaurants, cafés and bars clearly oriented to a queer clientele abound, with new book, video and adult-toy shops aimed at gays and lesbians continuing to reinvigorate the once falling-apart Chueca. Several gay- and lesbian-friendly hotels also operate around here.

Madrid's gay, lesbian and trans pride march (p29) is on the last Saturday in June, and if you're queer (and even if you're not), this is a riotously fun time to be in town. The bi-weekly *Shanguide* is jammed with listings and contact ads, while the *Mapa Gaya de Madrid* also has extensive listings. Both are available from **Berkana** (☎ 91 522 55 99; Calle de Hortaleza 64, Chueca).

BEST GAY MEETING PLACES
> Mamá Inés (p112)
> Café Acuarela (p108)
> Antigua Casa Ángel Sierra (p107)
> Susan Club (p113)
> Diurno (p109)

BEST GAY CLUBS
> Why Not? (p113)
> Local Café Bar Lounge (p113)
> Cool (pictured left; p56)

V

GREEN SPACES

The narrow lanes in central Madrid can be deceptive, because this is one of the greenest capital cities in Europe. An aerial photo of Madrid reveals vast expanses of greenery and, at ground level, every one of them provides a welcome respite from the noise, traffic and general clamour that can seem to assail you from every side.

Clearly some barrios are greener than others and it's no coincidence that the tree-lined streets of Chamberí and Salamanca are central Madrid's most livable (and hence most expensive) barrios. The Paseo de la Castellana (and the Paseo del Prado and Paseo de los Recoletos), which runs through central Madrid like a river, was in fact once a small creek on the eastern outskirts of Madrid and the abundance of trees that remain make this one of Europe's leafiest boulevards. From here, kilometres of foliage climb away to the east. Across town to the west, Madrid drops down from the Palacio Real and sweeps away to the west in a seemingly endless expanse of luxuriant green.

Green spaces such as these are magnets for Madrileños and when the weather's fine, the parks are as happily alive with people and street performers as anywhere in the city.

BEST PUBLIC PARKS
> Parque del Buen Retiro (p17)
> Parque del Oeste (p127)
> Casa del Campo via the Teleférico (p127)

BEST PUBLIC GARDENS
> Real Jardín Botánico (p86)
> Jardines de Sabatini (pictured; p15)
> La Rosaleda (Parque del Buen Retiro; p17)

LIVE MUSIC & FLAMENCO

Madrid's live-music scene has never been in better health. Yes, Madrid has become an increasingly important stopover for international stars on their European tours – some of these concerts are held at the Plaza de Toros Monumental de las Ventas (p90) – but Madrid's buzzing year-round music scene of jazz, flamenco and rock is what keeps its knowledgeable, music-loving public satisfied.

Flamenco in Madrid operates on two levels. First, the *tablaos* (flamenco venues with a dinner-and-floorshow programme) serve up a diet of high-quality flamenco most nights of the week. They're a wonderful introduction to the art. Remember, however, that Spanish flamenco aficionados are more likely to be found at more intimate venues where the flamenco music is raw and more spontaneous, or turning flamenco into a participation art by heading to nightclubs where DJs spin flamenco tunes.

Jazz is the other mainstay of the Madrid night. Although you may find venues elsewhere, Huertas is the spiritual home of jazz here with a host of intimate, crowded venues drawing international and local acts. Rock is more of a movable feast, with Chamberí home to Honky Tonk (p133) and Clamores (p133). Malasaña is, however, where they hold fast to rock of all description, beating out into the streets from just about any bar.

BEST FLAMENCO VIBE
> Cardamomo (p80)
> Villa Rosa (p81)
> Casa Patas (p69)
> El Juglar (p69)
> Almonte (p101)
> El Callejón (p78)

BEST LIVE JAZZ VENUES
> Café Central (p80)
> El Berlín Jazz Café (p55)
> Populart (pictured above; p80)
> Sol y Sombra (p81)
> El Junco Jazz Club (p112)

RESTAURANTS & CAFÉS

Madrid is a great place to eat out and the city's discerning diners ensure that only places of true quality last the distance. Spanish regional cooking is rightly famed around the world and restaurants serving cuisines from every corner of the country can be found in Madrid. In recent years the full range of international flavours has also become available as Spanish palates become more adventurous.

Malasaña and Chueca are where the greatest innovations are taking place, although La Latina, Lavapiés, Huertas and Chamberí aren't far behind. Salamanca, Paseo del Prado and El Retiro are usually about fine dining in sedate surrounds.

As important as the myriad tastes on offer, however, it's the buzz that accompanies eating in Madrid that elevates the city into the ranks of the great culinary capitals of the world. In Madrid, eating is not a functional pastime to be squeezed in between other more important tasks. Instead it's one of life's great pleasures to be enjoyed for hours on end with friends and a glass or two of wine.

As the capital of the Spanish-speaking world, Madrid was once littered with grand old literary cafés. Some of these survive around the Glorieta de Bilbao and along the Paseo de los Recoletos.

BEST FOR NOUVELLE CUISINE
> A Dos Velas (p118)
> Ene Restaurante (p65)
> La Musa (p121)
> Nina (p121)
> Taberna Matritum (p66)
> Bazaar (p105)
> El Original (p106)

BEST FOR HIGH-CLASS DINING
> Restaurante Sobrino de Botín (p51)
> Lhardy (p76)
> La Gastroteca de Santiago (p51)
> Sula (p100)
> Santceloni (p132)
> Sergi Arola Gastro (p132)

BEST VEGETARIAN
> La Isla del Tesoro (p120)
> El Estragón (p64)
> Al Natural (p49)
> Yerbabuena (p52)
> Restaurante Integral Artemisa (p77)

BEST GRAND OLD CAFÉS
> Café Comercial (p122)
> Gran Café de Gijón (p110)
> Café-Restaurante El Espejo (p108)
> El Parnasillo (p123)
> Café del Círculo de Bellas Artes (p53)

TAPAS

Going out for tapas – as a precursor to a meal, an accompaniment to drinking or a meal in itself – is perhaps the most appealing of all Spanish traditions, and Madrid is one of the great tapas capitals of Spain.

In San Sebastián or Sevilla you can expect your tapas to be dominated by local specialities, but the strength in Madrid's tapas lies in its variety. Every regional Spanish cuisine – especially Basque, Galician and Andalucian – can be found here, often in the same bar. Wash it down with a regional Spanish wine and Madrid will have you hooked.

Tapas in Madrid generally means either a selection of bite-sized morsels or *raciones*, a full plate loaded with tapas of the same variety. If you're in a bar serving the former, you can usually take a small plate and help yourself or point to the morsel you want. If you do this, it is customary to keep track of what you eat (by holding on to the toothpicks for example) and then tell the barman when it comes time to pay. If you particularly like something you can have a *media ración* (half ration) or even a full *ración* – most bars have menus listing what's available. In some bars you'll also get a small (free) tapa when you buy a drink.

If Spaniards have eaten a big meal at lunchtime, they may choose to *tapear* or *ir de tapeo* (go on a tapas crawl) in the evening. Sunday from around 1pm is another quintessentially Madrileño time to *tapear*.

BEST TAPAS SELECTION
> Casa Lucas (p64)
> Bocaito (p105)
> Los Gatos (p76)
> Juanalaloca (p65)
> Casa Alberto (p75)

BEST REGIONAL TAPAS
> Biotza (p96)
> Sagaretxe (p132)
> Txakolina (p66)
> La Trucha (p76)
> Maceiras (p76)

>BACKGROUND

REGE CAROLO III
ANNO
MDCCLXXVIII

Peer back through history, Puerta de Alcalá (p85)

BACKGROUND

HISTORY

Madrid's origins date back to the 9th century when much of the Iberian Peninsula came under the sway of Muslim Al-Andalus with its capital at Córdoba. With the Christian kingdoms of northern Spain scrambling to regain lost territory in what became known as the Reconquista (Reconquest), the emir of Córdoba, Muhammad I, built a chain of fortified positions in what is now central Spain. Among these was Magerit, or Mayrit, a name that comes from the Arabic word *majira*, meaning water channel. Thus was Madrid born as a Muslim garrison town in 854.

Across Iberia the armies of Muslim and Christian Spain battled for supremacy, but Magerit passed into Christian hands without a fight. In 1085, Toledo's ruler gave Magerit to King Alfonso VI of Castile in return for assistance in capturing Valencia.

The centuries that followed were obscure ones for Madrid, which played second fiddle to Segovia and Toledo. In 1309, the travelling Cortes (royal court and parliament) sat in Madrid for the first time, but the city's hesitant rise suffered a blow in 1348 when the Black Death devastated the population. Apart from serving as a base for royal hunting parties, Madrid was a backwater that bore no comparison with other major Spanish, let alone European, cities.

Despite its provincial status the city was chosen by Felipe II as the capital of Spain in 1561. It was an odd choice, with a smaller population (30,000) than Toledo, Seville and Valladolid. In truth, it was chosen precisely because it was an inoffensive city without its own power base that could threaten royal power. Felipe II also wanted the capital to be 'a city fulfilling the function of a heart located in the middle of the body'.

Royal patronage was kind to Madrid and by the 17th century a host of monumental buildings was rising amid the city's slums and the great artists of the age were flocking here. By the middle of the century the city was home to 175,000 people, making it the fifth-largest city in Europe.

It was Carlos III (r 1759–88) who transformed the place. Known as the 'Mayor of Madrid' for the attention he lavished on the capital, he cleaned up the city, embarked on a major road-building programme, inaugurated the Real Jardín Botánico and sponsored artists such as Goya and Tiepolo.

The French occupied Madrid in 1808 and Napoleon's brother, Joseph Bonaparte, was crowned king of Spain. Madrid did not take kindly to foreign rule and, on the morning of 2 May 1808, Madrileños attacked French troops around the Palacio Real and what is now Plaza del Dos de Mayo in Malasaña. By the end of the day the rebels were quashed. Joseph Bonaparte went on to transform Madrid with a host of measures necessary in a city that had grown up without any discernible sense of town planning.

After the French were expelled from Spanish soil in 1813, the city was in disarray and famines were the norm. Fernando VII returned as king in 1814 and did little to improve the lot of ordinary Madrileños, although he did leave behind the Parque del Buen Retiro and Museo del Prado.

By the middle of the 19th century, a building boom sparked by the re-possession of Church property saw Madrid's general infrastructure finally begin to match the grandeur of its major monuments. Street lighting was added and in 1910 work began on carving out Gran Vía. Nine years later the first Metro line started operation.

The 1920s were a period of frenzied activity, not just in urban construction but in intellectual life. As many as 20 newspapers circulated on the streets and writers and artists converged on the capital, which hopped to the sounds of American jazz.

However, dark clouds were gathering. Municipal elections in Madrid in April 1931 brought a coalition of republicans and socialists to power. At a national level, a second republic was proclaimed and Alfonso XIII fled. In July 1936 the civil war began, with devastating consequences for the city.

Having stopped nationalist troops advancing from the north, Madrid found itself in the sights of Franco's forces, who were moving up from the south. The government escaped to Valencia, but the city's defenders (a mix of hastily assembled recruits, sympathisers from the army and air force, the International Brigades and Soviet advisers) held firm. Fighting was heaviest in the northwest of the city around Argüelles, but Madrid kept Franco at bay for two and a half years, during which time Madrileños lived a bizarre reality. People went about their daily business, caught the Metro to work and got on with things as best they could. All the while, nationalist artillery intermittently shelled the city, particularly Gran Vía (which became known as 'Howitzer Alley'), from the Casa de Campo. On 28 March 1939, an exhausted Madrid finally surrendered.

Having taken the city, Franco and his right-wing Falangist Party maintained a heavy repression and Madrid in the early 1940s was impoverished and battle-scarred, a 'city of a million cadavers', according to one observer.

The dire state of the Spanish economy forced hundreds of thousands of starving *campesinos* (peasants) to flock to the capital, increasing the

BACKGROUND

already enormous pressure for housing. In the 1950s alone, more than 600,000 arrived from elsewhere in Spain.

By the early 1960s, the so-called *años de desarollo* (years of development) had largely replaced the *años de hambre* (years of hunger). But Madrileños never really warmed to Franco and an increased standard of living did little to diminish their disdain for a man who held the capital in an iron grip. From 1965, opposition to Franco's regime became steadily more vocal. In 1973 the Basque separatist group Euskadi Ta Askatascna (ETA) stunned the capital with the spectacular assassination of Admiral Carrero Blanco, Franco's prime minister and designated successor. Franco died on 20 November 1975. The country then returned to a monarchy under Juan Carlos I, who favoured a more open political system.

With democracy taking root, Madrid embraced its new-found freedom with gusto. An aborted coup attempt in February 1981 became a mere blip for a city becoming famous throughout Europe for *la movida madrileña* (literally 'the Madrid scene'), a decade-long party during which the city rocked, the arts flourished and nothing was taboo. What was remarkable about *la movida* is that it was presided over by Enrique Tierno Galván, an ageing former university professor affectionately known throughout Spain as 'the old teacher'. A Socialist, he became mayor in 1979 and, for many, launched *la movida* by telling a public gathering *'a colocarse y ponerse al loro'* (loosely translated, 'get stoned and do what's cool'). Not surprisingly, he was Madrid's most popular mayor ever and when he died in 1986, a million Madrileños turned out for his funeral. In 1992 Madrid was named Europe's cultural capital.

Madrid's burgeoning self-confidence was shaken on 11 March 2004 when 10 bombs exploded on four rush-hour commuter trains heading into Atocha station. When the dust cleared, 191 people had died and 1400 were wounded, many of them seriously. It was the biggest terror attack in the nation's history and it left the city deeply traumatised. Some 36 hours after the attacks, more than three million Madrileños streamed onto the streets to protest against the bombings – the largest demonstration in Madrid's history.

LIFE IN MADRID

Living as a Madrileño can be hard work. For one thing people in Madrid lead frenetic lives, working hard, playing even harder and all the while giving the impression of being quite relaxed about it all. Thus it is that

Madrileños by one estimate work longer hours and sleep less than almost any other Europeans.

There seems to be an unwritten rule that demands Madrileños spend a good part of their life outdoors and locals think nothing of spending an entire afternoon with friends in a *terraza* (outdoor bar). When the weather's fine, the chattering din continues until deep into the night, which helps make this one of the most agreeably noisy cities on the planet. Such a lifestyle is not restricted to the younger crop of Madrileños and you're almost as likely to stumble over football-playing ankle-biters or sprightly *abuelos* (grandparents) at midnight as run into drinking buddies.

Madrid is also transforming into one of Europe's most cosmopolitan cities. For decades home to immigrants from elsewhere in Spain, Madrid's population of non-Spanish immigrants doubled in the five years to 2004. By January 2009, almost 17.5% of Madrid's population was foreign-born, more than double the national average. The fact that it is almost impossible to find a true *gato* (Madrileño with two parents and two grandparents born in Madrid) is one reason why this city is one of the most open and tolerant cities in Spain.

Until the economic crisis, Spain was hurtling towards economic parity with the rest of Europe. Some key indicators of living standards, especially Spanish pay packets, still lag some distance behind and, after a decade of improving numbers, unemployment has risen alarmingly. And yet, even amid the worst economic downturn in a generation, Madrid still has a spring in its step. Many are doing it tough, but not that you'd notice. Just for good measure, Madrid has also launched a bid to host the 2016 Olympics.

One final thing: Madrileños can seem gruff and economical with etiquette. In short, they're not too fussed with 'please' and 'thank

DID YOU KNOW?

> Central Madrid population: 3.21 million
> Greater Madrid population: 5.37 million
> Madrid has the second-highest GDP in Spain, behind Catalonia
> Up to 75% of inward foreign investment into Spain is now directed at Madrid
> On average Madrileños earn around €2000 per month before tax, the highest in Spain
> Average house price in Madrid: €331,206
> Spain's unemployment rate: 17.4%; Madrid's unemployment rate: 15%
> Madrid has more trees than any other city in the world (around 500,000)
> Passengers using Madrid's Barajas Airport in 2008: 50.85 million

you'. But this rarely signifies unfriendliness – it's just a different way of doing things. There is one exception: blocking the left side of an escalator is one of the few ways in Madrid to make enemies.

GOVERNMENT & POLITICS

Three layers of government watch over Madrileños – municipal, regional and national.

The People's Party's (PP) Alberto Ruiz-Gallardón won the mayoral elections in May 2003. As *alcalde* (mayor), Ruiz-Gallardón has presided over an ambitious infrastructure and public works programme. Despite the epic levels of traffic and other transport disruption caused by the programme, Ruiz-Gallardón easily won re-election in 2007 and remains popular. Despite an ill-fated bid for a role in national politics at the 2008 elections, and his subsequent promise to resign as mayor, Ruiz-Gallardón has announced that he will again stand for mayor in 2011.

The Comunidad de Madrid, one of 17 Spanish autonomous regions, is led by the PP's Esperanza Aguirre who became Spain's first ever female regional president in October 2003; she increased her majority in 2007. Before moving into regional politics, Aguirre served as a senator – at the 1996 general elections she won 1.6 million votes, more than any other female senator in Spanish history – and as national education and culture minister in José María Aznar's first PP government.

Relations between Ruiz-Gallardón and Aguirre are said to be defined by professional cohabitation rather than close friendship.

ART & ARCHITECTURE
A PAINTING MASTER CLASS

Few cities in the world can match Madrid's pantheon of master painters who passed through and made the city their own.

The late 17th and 18th centuries are often referred to as the 'golden age' of Spanish art, as Spain's monarchs began to patronise the arts in a serious way. Most famously of all, Seville-born Diego Rodríguez de Silva y Velázquez (1599–1660) moved to Madrid as a court painter. Although famous for his landscapes, religious subjects and snapshots of everyday life, he is defined by the unrivalled vitality and humanity of his royal portraits.

Francisco José de Goya y Lucientes (1746–1828) dominated the 18th and early 19th centuries as powerfully as Velázquez had done almost 150 years before. After a less-than-auspicious start to his career – he came from a provincial family and began work as a cartoonist – he became deaf in 1792; many critics speculate that his condition was largely responsible for his wild, often merciless style that would become increasingly unshackled by convention. By 1799, Goya was appointed Carlos IV's court painter.

In the last years of the 18th century he painted enigmatic masterpieces such as *La Maja Vestida* (The Young Lady Dressed) and *La Maja Desnuda* (The Young Lady Undressed). The rumour mill suggests the subject was none other than the Duquesa de Alba, with whom he allegedly had an affair that scandalised Madrid society. The Inquisition was not amused and it ordered the paintings to be covered up. The prolific Goya then executed the playful frescoes in Madrid's Ermita de San Antonio de la Florida and produced *Los Caprichos* (The Caprices), a biting series of etchings lambasting the follies of court life and ignorant clergy.

War and the arrival of the French in 1808 had a profound impact on Goya. His *El Dos de Mayo* (The Second of May) and *El Tres de Mayo* (The Third of May) were unforgiving portrayals of the brutality of war and became iconic paintings of Madrid's history. After he retired to the Quinta del Sordo (Deaf Man's House) he created his nightmarish *Pinturas Negras* (Black Paintings).

FILM

> *Carne Trémula* (Live Flesh; 1997) – A typically kaleidoscopic Pedro Almodóvar love thriller starring Javier Bardem.
> *El Otro Lado de la Cama* (The Other Side of the Bed; 2002) – Riotously funny story of love among a group of 30-something Madrileños.
> *Historias del Kronen* (Stories From the Kronen; 1994) – A slightly depressing story of alienated urban youth in the heart of Madrid.
> *Laberinto de Pasiones* (Labyrinth of Passions; 1982) – Confirmed Almodóvar's status as an icon of 1980s Madrid with a cameo role by the director himself.
> *La Colmena* (The Beehive; 1982) – A compelling portrait of Madrid during the grey years of the 1950s.
> *La Comunidad* (Common Wealth; 2000) – Alex de la Iglesia's cheerfully off-the-wall tale of greed in a Madrid apartment block, starring Carmen Maura.
> *Los Fantasmas de Goya* (Goya's Ghosts; 2006) – Set in 1792 Madrid, this recent offering by Milos Forman tells the story of Goya, the Inquisition and the painter's many scandals.
> *Pepi, Luci, Bom, y las Otras Chicas del Montón* (Pepi, Luci, Bom and Other Girls on the Heap; 1980) – One of Almodóvar's earliest offerings that captures the craziness of Madrid during *la movida madrileña* (sociocultural movement following Francisco Franco's death).

If the late 17th and 18th centuries were Spain's golden age, then the 20th century was easily its rival. Málaga-born Pablo Ruiz Picasso (1881–1973) arrived in Madrid in 1897 for a year's study at the Escuela de Bellas Artes de San Fernando. Never one to allow himself to be confined within formal structures, the precocious Picasso took himself to the Prado to learn from the masters, and to the streets to depict life as he saw it. Picasso's extremely complex cubist form reached its highpoint in *Guernica*, which hangs in the Centro de Arte Reina Sofía.

Picasso was not the only artist who found the Escuela de Bellas Artes de San Fernando too traditional. In 1922 Salvador Dalí (1904–89) arrived in the city from Catalonia, but he quickly took to the cafés, music halls and brothels of Madrid. For four years, the three self-styled anarchists and bohemians Dalí, homosexual poet Federico García Lorca and future film-director Luis Buñuel romped through '20s Madrid, engaging in pranks, immersing themselves in jazz and taking part in endless *tertulias* (literary discussions). Dalí was finally expelled from art school and left Madrid, never to return. Lorca's poem *'Pequeño vals vienés'* was interpreted by Leonard Cohen as the song 'Take This Waltz', and the poet's statue stands in Plaza de Santa Ana in Sol.

Another Madrid name of note is Juan Gris (1887–1927), one of the principal exponents of the cubist style. His works can be seen in the Centro de Arte Reina Sofía and at the Real Academia de Bellas Artes de San Fernando.

ARCHITECTURE

When Felipe II established Madrid as Spain's capital in 1561, the 'city' was little more than a squalid ensemble of timber housing interspersed with the odd grand church or palace and laced with fetid lanes. The monumental Paseo del Prado, which now provides Madrid with so much of its grandeur, was nothing more than a small creek. Thus it was that the Romanesque and Gothic flourishes seen elsewhere in Europe largely passed Madrid by.

However, the Spanish capital can boast its own architectural style, which is known as *barroco madrileño* (Madrid baroque). This 16th-century fusion of a stern Renaissance style with a restrained approach to the ornamental baroque influences so popular elsewhere in Europe was largely the work of Juan de Herrera (1530–97), perhaps the greatest figure of the Spanish Renaissance. Madrid baroque's austere but graceful brick, stone and slate combinations are evident all across Los Austrias, the oldest quarter, with the Real Casa de la Panadería and the Ayuntamiento in the Plaza de la Villa among the signature works.

Neoclassicist architectural style transformed Madrid in the 18th century and it was Juan de Villanueva (1739–1811) who left Madrid's most famous neoclassical landmark, the Palacio de Villanueva that houses the Museo del Prado.

The outpouring of creativity that accompanied the dawn of the 20th century, known to many as the *belle époque*, also left its mark. Headed by the prolific Antonio Palacios (1874–1945), architects from all over Spain began to transform Madrid into the airy city you see today. Palacios' Palacio de Comunicaciones on Plaza de la Cibeles was completed in 1917 and is the most eye-catching monument of this period.

International architectural circles are buzzing with the unprecedented energy and innovation surrounding contemporary Spanish architecture. The impact upon Madrid has been muted, although the Caixa Forum building along Paseo del Prado is a stunning exception.

FURTHER READING

> *A Travellers Companion to Madrid* (2005; Hugh Thomas) – A fascinating compendium of extracts about Madrid from the great and good.
> *Atlas Ilustrado de la Historia de Madrid* (2004; Pedro López Carcelén) – Charts Madrid's growth into a modern metropolis using historical maps.
> *Ghosts of Spain* (2006; Giles Tremlett) – A journey through 20th-century Spain by the *Guardian's* Madrid correspondent.
> *Goya* (2006; Robert Hughes) – The definitive guide to Madrid's most intriguing artistic personality.
> *Guernica – The Making of a Painting* (1985; Joaquín de la Puente) – The story behind one of the 20th century's best-known paintings.
> *A Heart So White* (2002; Javier Marías) – A subtle tale of family intrigue set in Madrid.
> *A Load of Bull – An Englishman's Adventures in Madrid* (2006; Tim Parfitt) – A fun, easy read about coming to terms, and then falling in love, with Madrid.
> *Madrid* (2001; Elizabeth Nash) – An informative and joyfully written account of the city's past and present.
> *Hidden Madrid: A Walking Guide* (2007; Mark & Peter Besas) – A quirky collection of anecdotes and curiosities about historical Madrid.
> *The New Spaniards* (2006; John Hooper) – Recently updated and highly readable account of 20th-century Spain.
> *Travesuras de la Niña Mala* (*That Bad Girl*; 2006; Mario Vargas Llosa) – An intercontinental love story that passes through the 1980s Lavapiés.
> *Winter in Madrid* (2006; Clive Sansom) – A page-turning thriller-cum-love-story set partly in Madrid during the civil war.

DIRECTORY
TRANSPORT
ARRIVAL & DEPARTURE
AIR

Madrid's **Barajas Airport** (☎ 902 404 704; www.aena.es) lies 15km northeast of the city.

The airport has four terminals. T1, T2 and T3 are part of the same complex; T4 is separate but is connected to the other three terminals by a regular shuttle bus. The easiest way to get to the airport is Line 8 of Madrid's Metro. T1, T2 and T3 are accessed via the 'Aeropuerto' station (one-way €2). For T4, the station is 'Aeropuerto T4' (one-way €2). If you're travelling on a 10-trip '10 Viajes Metrobús'

ticket (€7.40), you pay a €1 supplement for the airport.

GETTING AROUND

Madrid is a relatively compact city and the excellent Metro system can help you maximise your time and provide respite for weary legs. Throughout this book, the nearest Metro station is noted after the Ⓜ icon in each listing.

TRAVEL PASSES

In addition to the 10-trip Metrobús ticket (see opposite), you should also consider the **Abono Transportes Turísticos** (Tourist Travel Pass; www.metromadrid.es; adult 1-/2-/3-/7-day ticket €5.20/8.80/11.60/23.60, children under 11yr half price), which allows unlimited travel on any public transport.

TRAVEL TO/FROM THE AIRPORT

	Taxi	Bus	Metro
Pick-up point	outside arrivals hall	outside arrivals hall	in T2 & T4; follow signs from arrivals hall
Drop-off point	outside departures hall	outside departures hall	Aeropuerto station (T1, T2 & T3) or Aeropuerto T4 station (both Line 8)
Duration to centre	20min (45min in rush hour)	30 min (60min in rush hour)	20min to 30 min to Nuevos Ministerios Metro station
Cost to centre	€15-23 (incl €5.50 airport supplement)	€1	€1 (T1, T2 & T3), €2 (T4)
Frequency	n/a	every 15 min 5.30am-11.30pm	every 3 to 15min 6.05am-2am
Contact	n/a	www.emtmadrid.es	www.metromadrid.es

ALTERNATIVE ROUTES TO MADRID

Travelling to Madrid by train allows you to see so much more, as well as minimising your impact upon the environment. Madrid is well connected by train to most other European cities. From London, **Eurostar** (www.eurostar.com) gets you to Paris where trains connect to Madrid, thereby allowing you to visit two of Europe's most exciting cities in one trip. Two interesting alternatives from the UK are the passenger ferries operated by **Brittany Ferries** (www.brittanyferries.co.uk) from Plymouth to Santander or by **P&O European Ferries** (www.poportsmouth.com) from Portsmouth to Bilbao; from both Bilbao and Santander there are regular train services to Madrid.

From Morocco, ferries run from Tangier to Algeciras and Tarifa, or from Nador to Almería, where there are regular train connections to Madrid.

Tickets can be purchased online or at train stations, *estancos* (tobacconists) and newspaper kiosks in Madrid.

METRO

Metro de Madrid (☎ 902 444 403; www.metromadrid.es) is the fastest and most efficient way to navigate Madrid. Central Madrid has 11 colour-coded lines and operates from about 6am to around 2am.

Metrobús one-/10-trip tickets cost €1/7.40 and can be purchased at stations, *estancos* (tobacconists) and newspaper kiosks.

BUS

Buses operated by **Empresa Municipal de Transportes de Madrid** (EMT; ☎ 902 507 850; www.emtmadrid.es) travel along most city routes regularly between 6.30am and 11.30pm. Twenty-six night-bus routes *(búhos, or líneas nocturnas)* operate from midnight

to 6am from Plaza de la Cibeles. Metrobús tickets (left) are also valid on buses.

CERCANÍAS

The short-range *cercanías* regional trains are handy for making a quick, north–south hop between Chamartín and Atocha train stations (stopping at Nuevos Ministerios and Sol en route).

Tickets can be purchased at any train station for €1.20. *Cercanías* trains run from around 5.45am until midnight.

TAXI

You can pick up a cab at ranks throughout town or simply flag one down. Flag fall is €2.05, more after 10pm; make sure the meter is on. Several supplementary charges apply, such as €5.50 to/from the airport and €2.95 from cab ranks at train and bus stations.

TRANSPORT WITHIN MADRID

	Sol	La Latina	Huertas	Paseo del Prado
Sol	N/A	Walk 10min	Walk 10min	Metro 10min
La Latina	Walk 10min	N/A	Walk 10min	Metro 15-20 mins
Huertas	Walk 10min	Walk 10-15min	N/A	Walk 10min
Paseo del Prado	Metro 10min	Metro 15-20min	Metro 10min	N/A
Salamanca	Metro 15min	Metro 15min	Metro 15min	Metro 10-15 min
Chueca	Metro 10min	Metro 15min	Metro 15min	Walk 10-15min
Malasaña	Metro 10min	Metro 15-20min	Metro 15min	Metro 15-20 min
Chamberí	Metro 15min	Metro15-20min	Metro 20min	Metro 15-20min

Radio-Teléfono Taxi (☎ 91 547 82 00; www.radiotelefono-taxi.com in Spanish) and **Tele-Taxi** (☎ 91 371 21 31; www.tele-taxi.es) are 24-hour taxi services. Most taxi companies have *eurotaxi*, which are adapted for wheelchair users.

PRACTICALITIES
BUSINESS HOURS

Standard working hours are Monday to Friday from 8am or 9am to 2pm and then again from 3pm or 4pm for another three hours.

Banks Open from 8.30am to 2pm Monday to Friday; some also open 4pm to 7pm Thursday and/or 9am to 1pm Saturday.

Central post office Open from 8.30am to 9.30pm Monday to Saturday. Some branches open 8.30am to 8.30pm but most only 8am to 2pm Monday to Friday.

Restaurants Open from 1pm to 4pm and 8.30pm to midnight; later on Friday and Saturday.

Shops Open from 10am to 2pm and 5pm to 8pm Monday to Saturday; larger stores open 10am to 10pm Monday to Saturday. Some shops (especially in downtown Madrid and book and music stores) open on Sunday; all shops may open on the first Sunday of each month and throughout December.

DISCOUNTS

The **International Student Identity Card** (ISIC; www.isic.org) and the **Euro<26 card** (www.euro26.org), for youth under 26, are available from most national student organisations (for a fee) and entitle you discounted access to sights.

The **Madrid Card** (☎ 91 360 47 72; www.madridcard.com; 1/2/3 days €45/58/72, 3-day child's ticket €34) includes free entry to more than 50 attractions in and around Madrid and free Descubre Madrid walking tours (p167), as well as other discounts on public transport. You save

Salamanca	Chueca	Malasaña	Chamberí
Metro 15min	Metro 10min	Metro 10min	Metro 15min
Metro 15min	Metro 15min	Metro 15-20min	Metro 15-20min
Metro 15min	Metro 15min	Metro 15min	Metro 20min
Metro 10-15min	Walk 10-15min	Metro 15-20min	Metro 15-20min
N/A	Metro 10min	Metro 15-20 min	Metro 15-20min
Metro 10min	N/A	Walk 10min	Metro 5-10min
Metro 15-20min	Walk 10min	N/A	Walk 10min
Metro 15-20min	Metro 5-10min	Walk 10min	N/A

5% off the Madrid Card price by purchasing online. Otherwise, purchase it at the tourist offices on Plaza Mayor and in Calle del Duque de Medinaceli (see p168), and in some tobacconists, newspaper kiosks and hotels.

ELECTRICITY
The electric current in Madrid is 220V, 50Hz, as in the rest of Continental Europe. Several countries outside Europe (such as the USA and Canada) use 110V, 60Hz, which means that it's safest to use a transformer. Plugs have two round pins, as in the rest of Continental Europe.

EMERGENCIES
To report thefts, go to the **Servicio de Atención al Turista Extranjero** (Foreign Tourist Assistance Service; Map p42, C2; ☎ 91 548 85 37; Calle de Leganitos 19; ✆ 9am-10pm; Ⓜ Plaza de España or Santo Domingo) run by the Policía Nacional.
Ambulance (☎ 061)
EU standard emergency number (☎ 112)
Fire Brigade (Bomberos; ☎ 080)
Local Police (Policía Municipal; ☎ 092)
National Police (Policía Nacional; ☎ 091)

HOLIDAYS
Año Nuevo (New Year's Day) 1 January
Reyes (Epiphany or Three Kings' Day) 6 January
Jueves Santo (Holy Thursday) March/April
Viernes Santo (Good Friday) March/April
Fiesta del Trabajo (Labour Day) 1 May
Fiesta de la Comunidad de Madrid 2 May
Fiestas de San Isidro 15 May
La Asunción (Feast of the Assumption) 15 August
Día de la Hispanidad (Spanish National Day) 12 October
Todos los Santos (All Saints' Day) 1 November
Día de la Virgen de la Almudena 9 November
Día de la Constitución (Constitution Day) 6 December

CLIMATE CHANGE & TRAVEL

Travel – especially air travel – is a significant contributor to global climate change. At Lonely Planet, we believe that all who travel have a responsibility to limit their personal impact. As a result, we have teamed with Rough Guides and other concerned industry partners to support Climate Care, which allows people to offset the greenhouse gases they are responsible for with contributions to energy-saving projects and other climate-friendly initiatives in the developing world. Lonely Planet offsets all staff and author travel.

For more information, turn to the responsible travel pages on www.lonelyplanet .com. For details on offsetting your carbon emissions and a carbon calculator, go to www .climatecare.org.

La Inmaculada Concepción (Feast of the Immaculate Conception) 8 December
Navidad (Christmas) 25 December

INTERNET

A Tapear! (www.atapear.com, in Spanish) Reviews of more than 400 tapas bars in Madrid.
EsMadrid.com (www.esmadrid.com) The Ayuntamiento's (Town Hall's) website is outstanding, with events listings and detailed information on the city.
Mad About Madrid (www.madaboutmadrid .com) Comprehensive site with blogs, history and advice on exploring the city.
Turismo Madrid (www.turismomadrid.es) Portal of the regional Madrid tourist office with plenty of interesting links.

MONEY

The currency of Madrid is the euro (€). Central Madrid abounds with banks, and credit cards can be used in ATMs displaying the appropriate sign. Exchange offices are open for longer hours but generally offer poorer rates. Major cards, such as Visa, Visa Electron, MasterCard, Maestro and Cirrus, are accepted

throughout Madrid. When using these you'll need to show some form of photo ID (eg passport).

COSTS

Madrid is cheaper than most northern European cities, although it's fast catching up. The exception is the *menú del día*, a fixed-price, all-in set lunch that can cost under €10. Public transport, taxis and museum admission fees are cheap compared with most other Euro-

EXCHANGE RATES

Australia	A$1	€0.57
Canada	C$1	€0.62
Hong Kong	HK$1	€0.09
Japan	Y100	€0.76
New Zealand	NZ$1	€0.45
Singapore	S$1	€0.49
Switzerland	SFr1	€0.66
UK	UK£1	€1.16
USA	US$1	€0.72

pean cities. Leaving aside your accommodation and any purchases you might make, expect to spend on average €40 to €60 per day.

NEWSPAPERS & MAGAZINES

Most major European dailies are available at newspaper kiosks throughout Madrid; a few international magazines are also available. The *International Herald Tribune* includes an eight-page supplement of articles from *El País* translated into English.

The major Spanish dailies are the left-leaning *El Publico,* centre-left *El País,* the centre-right *El Mundo* and the conservative-right *ABC*. *Marca* is devoted exclusively to sport, while free morning dailies include *20 Minutos, ADN* and *¡Que!*.

In addition to the widely available publications with events listings (see p25), on Friday pick up *El Mundo's* supplement magazine, *Metropoli* (in Spanish), for information on the week's offerings.

ORGANISED TOURS

Adventurous Appetites (☎ 639 331 073; www.adventurousappetites.com; 4-hr tours from €50; 🕗 8pm Mon-Sat) English-language tapas tours.

Bike Spain (☎ 91 559 06 53; www.bike spain.info; per person €30) Guided two-wheel tours of Madrid.

Descubre Madrid (Discover Madrid; ☎ 91 588 29 06; www.esmadrid.com/descubrema

drid; walking tours for adult/under 25yr, student or senior €3.90/3.12) Around a dozen excellent themed walking tours in Spanish and English run by the Centro de Turismo de Madrid.

Urban Movil (☎ 91 542 77 71, 687 535 443; www.urbanmovil.com; Calle Mayor 78; 1-/2-hr tour per person €40/65) Tours through central Madrid aboard a two-wheel, stand-up Segway; prices include 10-minute training.

TELEPHONE

The international country code for Spain is ☎ 34.

The blue-and-yellow payphones accept coins, *tarjetas telefónicas* (phonecards) issued by the national phone company Telefónica and, in some cases, credit cards. Cut-rate *tarjetas telefónicas* can be bought from *estancos* and newsstands in central Madrid.

The Spanish mobile (cellular) phone system operates on the GSM 900 system although an increasing number operate at GSM 1800 or 3G 2100. Check with your mobile provider as things change rapidly.

USEFUL PHONE NUMBERS

The regional Oficina de Turismo website (www.turismomadrid.es) has a list of numbers under the 'General Information' tab.

Domestic operator ☎ 1009 (including *llamada por cobro revertido,* reverse-charge calls).

English-speaking Spanish international operator ☎ 1008 (calls within Europe or for Morocco).

English-speaking Spanish international operator ☎ 1005 (rest of the world).
International direct dial code ☎ 00.
International directory inquiries ☎ 11825.
Local directory inquiries ☎ 11818.

TIPPING

In restaurants, most Madrileños leave small change or around €1 per person. Tipping taxi drivers is not common practice, although rounding up is appreciated. You should tip the porter €2 to €5 at higher-class hotels.

TOURIST INFORMATION

Centro de Turismo de Madrid (☎ 91 588 16 36; www.esmadrid.com; Plaza Mayor 27; 🕒 9.30am-8.30pm; **M** Sol) Outstanding Ayuntamiento (Town Hall) tourist office on the north side of the Plaza Mayor with free access to its city database, organised tours, free downloads of the metro map to your mobile and helpful staff.
Oficina de Turismo (☎ 902 100 007, 91 429 49 51; www.turismomadrid.es; Calle del Duque de Medinaceli 2; 🕒 8am-8pm Mon-Sat, 8am-2pm Sun; **M** Banco de España) Run by the regional Comunidad de Madrid government.

TRAVELLERS WITH DISABILITIES

Although things are changing slowly, Madrid remains something of an obstacle course for travellers with a disability. Metro lines built since the late 1990s generally have elevators for wheelchair access but the older lines tend to be ill-equipped. The single-deck *piso bajo* buses have no steps inside and, in some cases, have ramps that can be used by people in wheelchairs. For information on taxis for disabled travellers, see p164.

Throughout this book, sights, shops, restaurants and nightclubs with wheelchair access are marked with the ♿ icon.

INFORMATION & ORGANISATIONS

For guided tours for travellers with a disability, as well as a list of wheelchair-friendly hotels, restaurants and museums, click on the 'Madrid Accesible' (Spanish only) link on the Madrid tourist office website (www.esmadrid.com).
Access-able Travel Source (☎ 303-232 2979; www.access-able.com; USA)
Accessible Travel & Leisure (☎ 014-5272 9739; www.accessibletravel.co.uk; UK)
Holiday Care (☎ 084-5124 9971; www .holidaycare.org.uk; Shap Rd, Kendal, Cumbria LA9 6NZ, UK)
ONCE (☎ 91 436 53 00; www.once.es; Calle de José Ortega y Gasset 22-24; **M** Núñez de Balboa) The Spanish association for the blind. You may be able to get hold of a Madrid guide in Braille, although it's not published every year.
Royal Association for Disability & Rehabilitation (Radar; ☎ 020-7250 3222; www.radar.org.uk; 12 City Forum, 250 City Rd, London, EC1V 8AF, UK)

>INDEX

See also separate subindexes for See (p172), Shop (p173), Eat (p173), Drink (p175) and Play (p175).

000 map pages

INDEX

000 map pages

000 map pages